FOUR SONS OF NORWAY

Four Sons of Norway

HELEN ACKER

Illustrated by Nils Hogner

Biography Index Reprint Series

BOOKS FOR LIBRARIES PRESS
FREEPORT, NEW YORK

STANDARD BOOK NUMBER:

8369-8010-7

LIBRARY OF CONGRESS CATALOG CARD NUMBER:

72-117318

PRINTED IN THE UNITED STATES OF AMERICA

To my nephews

Jacky, Tommy, Jimmy, and Peter

ACKNOWLEDGMENTS

Acknowledgment is hereby made, and thanks expressed, to the following firms:

American-Scandinavian Foundation, for approximately 279 words from *Edvard Grieg*, by David Monrad Johansen; and approximately two hundred words from *Saga of Fridtjof Nansen*, by Jon Sörensen.

Dodd, Mead & Company, Inc., for 133 words from *Grieg and His Music*, by Henry T. Finck, copyright, 1909, 1936 by A. H. C. Finck.

Harper & Brothers, for approximately three hundred words from *Farthest North*, by Fridtjof Nansen.

Henry Holt and Company, Inc., for twenty-three words from *Ibsen the Master Builder*, by Adolf Edward Zucker.

W. W. Norton & Company, Inc., for approximately 119 words, from *The Life of Ibsen*, by Halvdan Koht.

Princeton University Press, for 141 words from *Life of Ole Bull*, by Mortimer Smith.

Charles Scribner's Sons, for thirty words from *Henrik Ibsen*, by Edmund Goss.

CONTENTS

ILLUSTRATIONS

THE STORY OF OLE BULL

OLE BULL

1810–1880

About a hundred years ago, Norway was a poor and small nation. For four hundred years she had been ruled by Denmark. Danish writers, and Danish artists, and Danish musicians told the world outside of life among the Scandinavian nations. And then, in 1814, the people of Norway became independent. It was a difficult time for the small country. The people had to build up their own national life, their own literature, their own music and arts.

In this time of beginning, the morning in the life of the nation, came their first great man. He was Ole Bull who played on a wonderful singing violin. He was like a troubador, and by his music carried abroad the name and fame of his country.

CHAPTER I

A GIFT

In all the vast world of lands and seas, there is probably no country anywhere as beautiful as the west coast of Norway. It is a wonderland of islands, mountains, and those winding arms of the sea which are called fjords. The fjords often lead inland for more than a hundred miles. They reach into narrow mountain valleys where the mountains are like great towers, and where there are all manner of waterfalls. Some of these are great and boisterous and fall in a crash of thunder, while others are like clouds of mist, delicate, gauzy, and fairylike.

Toward the southern end of this beautiful coast, at the head of a narrow and winding fjord, there is the old city of Bergen. Bergen is one of the most interesting cities in the world, both because of its great natural picturesqueness, and because it has kept, in its old buildings and wharfs and trading houses, much of the atmosphere of the old days. Seven mountains stand at its back, many islands crowd its harbor, and the rains and mists that veil it on most of the days of the year add to the feeling of legend.

One gray afternoon in the year 1815, on a typically Bergen day of heavy mists, a tall man might have been seen walking through the old section of the city. He wore galoshes, raincoat, and cap, and he carried under his arm a large package. Whatever the package was, he appeared in no hurry to deliver it. He walked in a leisurely manner, looking around him as though he enjoyed what he saw. The street was the ancient one called the Tykesbrigge. On one side were the wharfs and the fishing boats; and on the other, there still stood some of the medieval buildings that had been built by the German Hanseatic League traders. The man stopped in front of the doorway of one of these old buildings. Above the door was a figure of a butcher cut out of wood. In one hand this butcher held an axe with which to kill or cut up fish.

"Curious and interesting," the man was thinking. "The arts of the old days are still here with us. This wooden butcher was probably carved in a German village by the town's wood carver. I wish I had my nephew here with me to look at him. How the boy likes these streets, the boats, the fisherman talk, the fish smells, and all these old alleys filled with barrels and kegs! There's only one thing he likes better than looking at the sights, and picking up a herring or two from the fish barrels."

The tall man smiled. Then he looked down at the package that he carried and carefully changed it from one arm to the other. "I think the thing the boy likes best in the world is here in this box. The trolls take me for delaying so long."

He began to walk rapidly. He was going to the home of his sister, Fru Anna Bull, and the box was a present for the small nephew of whom he had been talking. "Was there ever such a fine boy?" he thought. "A real little Norwegian, only five years old, but straight as a candle and lively as a little trout."

The tall man turned into a street of comfortable-looking houses, and after a few minutes more of walking, he came to the large house of his sister. Inside, the lamps were already lighted, and, in the mist, the house looked cheerful and inviting. He pushed open the door.

"Ho, there!" he called. "Hi, Ole! Ole Bull, come here."

But it was his sister who came in first. "Oh, it's you, Jens," she said. "Sit down. Ole is upstairs with his grandmother. He is begging for stories of Norway. How the child loves the old tales! Valhalla, Odin, Thor, Norns, trolls, dwarfs—he can't have enough of them. When she sings songs, especially those queer songs of the mountain people, he can't restrain himself. He gets quite wild with excitement."

Jens nodded. "Yes, I know," he said.

At this moment, the boy, who had heard his uncle's voice, came running into the room. Ole Bull was a handsome little boy, tall for his five years, sturdily built. He had brown eyes, and light brown hair. He was smiling broadly, but was out of breath from the running.

"Ole," said Uncle Jens, "what took you so long? I've brought you a present, a big package. Don't you want it?"

But Ole was so out of breath from the running that he could not answer.

"Here it is," went on Uncle Jens. "You see, it's a big one."

Ole looked from his uncle to the package and back again. He smiled and his eyes lighted up. "What is it?" he asked.

14

"Well, find out," answered Uncle Jens. "You can take off the paper wrappings by yourself, I think."

When one is five years old, any present at all is wonderful, and the boy began to pull away the thick layer of paper that covered the package. It was well wrapped and the opening took some minutes, but at last, after all the layers of paper had been removed, there was disclosed a tiny violin, yellow as a lemon, fitted neatly in a small dark case.

Little Ole Bull stood perfectly still and stared. His eyes grew dark and sober, and in his chest his heart began to race. Several moments passed in complete silence. Then Ole touched the tiny violin with one hand, and finding it real and firm to the touch, he picked it up and stroked it and loved it and kissed it, all the while smiling, and beaming, and looking as though he were in heaven.

"Well, shall I tune it for you?" Uncle Jens asked, moved by the excitement of the boy. "Let me take it and tighten the strings."

But Ole would not let the violin get out of his hands. He sat down with it and tried to turn the screws himself, but they were stiff and would not yield to his hand. When he saw that he could not turn them, he took the violin to his mother, and, still holding it tightly, asked her to tighten the screws. When this was done, he picked it up and placed the violin on his shoulder. Then, to the great astonishment of his uncle and his mother, he took the bow, and holding it correctly, drew it over the strings so that there came from the little violin some clear and true notes. When he heard the notes, Ole could not contain himself. He tried other notes, and, after each sound, he listened and laughed with joy. In a few minutes, he tried the simple tune that his grandmother had been singing to him. When he heard this song coming from the yellow violin, his delight was so great that he stopped playing, and jumped up and down again and again. He hugged and kissed the tiny instrument in his arms.

"Good for you, little Ole," exclaimed Jens. "That is fine, really wonderful. So you like the fiddle? Can you put it away now in the case? You see, it must fit exactly. The case is made for it."

The boy put the case on the floor and carefully laid the little violin in place. Then he sat down on the floor by it and kept his hands on it.

"Do you know, Ole," said Jens, "it is a long time since I have known that you liked music. When you were small, only a baby, you know, I found you in the meadow one day. Do you know what you were doing? You were sitting in the grass holding a bluebell. You were looking at it intently. You told me that you could hear the tiny bell ring, and that the grass all around was singing, too, in a chorus of fine voices."

Uncle Jens looked at the boy on the floor, and Ole laughed at the story. "Oh, and I can tell you more than that," said Jens quickly, "when you were three, you were just big enough to fit into the case of my big violoncello. So, I put you in and gave you a candy to be quiet. Then I began to play. Soon, the case couldn't hold you any longer. Oh, no, out you danced, your eyes shining, and your feet beating out the time. Then you'd take up something, any-thing at all—a box, or a book and a yardstick—and there you would be playing away, hearty and merry, scraping the stick over the book, and thinking you were really making as fine music as the best of us."

At this moment in Uncle Jens's story, Ole's father came in. He was Johan Storm Bull, the apothecary for the town of Bergen, a handsome, vigorous, and successful man. When he saw Ole sitting on the floor, and holding so lovingly the small violin case, he frowned. He had set his heart on making a student of his first son, perhaps a preacher, the pastor of a congregation. Knowing that Ole was always imagining that he heard music and that he could make music himself, Johan Bull did not wish to encourage this interest which would lead away from serious study.

"You have brought a violin?" he said. "But soon Ole is to begin studies at the school. I think for him the music must wait."

"There is time for both, surely," said Jens.

"Perhaps," said Johan Bull. "I do not know. If the playing is done after school, it is well. But if the studies suffer, then music must wait."

Fru Anna interrupted. "Johan, Ole can already play a little. He took up the new violin, and he could almost play the folk song that Grandmother always sings."

"Can he indeed? Well, that is surprising and good," said Johan. "If Ole keeps the playing to the proper hours, I can have no objection."

There was no further talk of the violin and music. Supper was ready, and the whole family went in to sit down around the table. The scene was pleasant. Grandmother, Uncle Jens, Fru Anna, Johan Bull, and three boys, Ole, the eldest, and two small brothers, Randulf and Jens.

They ate boiled potatoes and fried fish. There was milk in a large brown jug, goat cheese, a hard bread, flat and round like little wheels, a red jam, made from cloudberries, picked in the mountain valleys, coffee, and a hasty pudding with raspberry sauce.

Jens left after the good supper. Outside the mists had turned into rain, and this rain was like a net over the town. Jens enjoyed the homeward walk. The streets and rooftops gleamed in the luminous dark. In the harbor, the many boats were rocking, and in the cafés the fishermen talked of the next day's catch. The mountains and the fjord were invisible in the rain, and the town had a snugness and smallness that were good and comfortable to Jens. His thoughts when they went from the rainy scene before him were of his nephew.

"It will be very interesting," he thought, "to see what the boy will do with the violin. I think it was quite remarkable what he did tonight."

Uncle Jens was almost home. The rain was coming faster, and threatened to become a heavy storm. "I must get in," he thought. "A book and a pipe will end the day for me."

So Jens went into his house and enjoyed both book and pipe and his thoughts of the evening. If it had been possible for him to look into his sister's house, he would have enjoyed yet more a scene that was taking place there. Little Ole had long since been sent to bed, but at this moment he was sitting by the bedroom window in his long nightdress. He was also looking at the roofs of Bergen, listening to the storm, and trying to reproduce some of the storm sounds on the tiny yellow violin that he held in his arms.

18

CHAPTER 2

AN ODD ADVENTURE

One day, a few weeks after little Ole Bull had his first
violin, he went for a walk with it under his arm. The mists
and rain had gone away, leaving a bright sky of peculiarly
soft and melting blue. Ole held the violin carefully. When
he skipped a step or two, he took particular care to support
it, to keep it secure from bumping and jouncing. The little
fiddle looked beautiful in the sunshine. It looked to Ole
as though it were smiling and coaxing to be taken along.
Ole walked briskly. It was pleasant to be walking in this
way. One simply could not be lonely with such a beautiful
little fiddle. If he wished, he could stop at any moment and
let it sing. It was odd, but Ole did not think of himself as
playing the fiddle. He thought of it as singing songs to him.

When Ole came to the corner of the street, he took the
turn that would lead him down to the harbor. This was
where there were the most interesting sights of Bergen—
the boats and the harbor, the fishermen, and the huge piles
of fish spread out for sale in the famous fish market. A few
minutes walking brought him to the fascinating scene.
There it was, spread out before his eyes, Bergen harbor,
crowded with small wooden docks which swarmed with

19

fishermen. Standing around were huge casks of fish, and there were so many boats that the harbor was like a forest with all the masts. Many of the fishermen wore interesting red pointed caps, high boots, and sea clothes. They were from the northern coasts of Norway, from the province called Nordland. Ole particularly liked these fishermen. They liked to talk and tell stories, and Ole had found that he had only to sit down and wait patiently for a while, and then soon the talk would get started.

Across the street from the wharves and boats were rows of shops. These buildings were very old. Because of their age, they were black in appearance, oddly built, with all sorts of passageways and funny gabled roofs and dark rooms. Many of these shops sold fish; others were cafés for the fishermen, or places selling food. Nearly all had a deep keg of pickled herring. These kegs fascinated all the visiting boys. There was that tantalizing smell, the dark brown vinegar and herring smell. In some cases, when the boys went too close, and sometimes so far forgot themselves as to dip into the dark brown keg, the owner would shriek out, "Begone, you trolls, I'll put you in a pickle too."

Then the boys would run, half frightened, yet half liking it, enjoying the threat and the chase among the old buildings, the casks and the kegs.

Ole was too little to take part in these last adventures. At this moment, he was choosing where to go with his fiddle, where to sit and watch. It was important to choose carefully. Some of the fishermen would be in a hurry and would pay no attention, but there were others who would like to talk and spin out wonderful tales of the sea and the storms and the adventures of the sail down the coast to

Ole played a tune to the fisherman.

Bergen. As Ole stood watching, the problem was decided. An old man spoke to him. He was from Nordland, Ole saw that at once from his pointed red cap.

"Let the fiends take me!" the old fisherman exclaimed, looking with curiosity at Ole's little fiddle. "I never saw the like in all my days. Can it be played?"

Ole nodded and held the fiddle up in the sunlight for the old man to see.

"We have a fiddler where I come from," the old man said. "But he is old. He plays at Christmas, then goes to sleep like a bear."

"Do you know any stories?" Ole asked.

The man from Nordland moved a keg from where it stood in the shadow of his boat over into the bright sunlight. He regarded Ole for a moment, then sat down on the keg and pulled his red cap down to his eyebrows. He began talking at once.

"In the north," he said, "each kind of fish has a king. Did you know that? Each king wears a golden crown. And do you know that the whales have waterspouts on their backs? Some spout higher than the houses. Those are interesting things beyond a doubt." He stopped a moment, smiling at Ole, then continued. "We have the people of Lapland for neighbors. They keep herds of reindeer. I know a Lapp boy smaller than you. He has a reindeer to pet and gives it salt in a little dish."

The fisherman lighted his pipe and sent puffs of smoke up into the air.

"Some of our islands in the north," he went on, "are covered with birds like a blanket. Have you seen that? In winter, we have not day, only night. We sit by the fire and prepare the tackle for the summer fishing. I have a little house on the side of a mountain. It has an iron stove which I found in a wreck. It is cozy on my mountain, I can tell you. I could not live on the flat land. And that's all I know. It's your turn now. Let me hear the little fiddle."

The old fisherman smiled at Ole; and Ole, smiling back, stood up straight and placed the fiddle on his shoulder. He played a little march, simple and lively, a tune that he had often heard. Then as he thought of the fisherman's story of the fishes with the king of each kind wearing a crown, an odd song came to his mind. So he played it too, the notes coming to him as fast as he played.

"Good, good!" exclaimed the fisherman. "Fine!"

Ole laughed and stroked the little fiddle and put it again carefully under his arm. The two sat talking in the sunshine for some time longer. Ole never tired of hearing the fishermen talk, and this old Nordlander was a rare one. Ole sat on the dock, cross-legged, holding the violin carefully, and the fisherman rocked on his keg as he talked. All around them the life on the quays went on, the unloading of the fish boats, the buying and selling, the talking and shouting.

The sky overhead continued to be clear, of the same soft melting Norwegian blue.

But the fisherman had his work to do, and Ole had to go home. He decided to take the long way. The long way was a whole excursion in itself. It took Ole and his violin along the harbor's edge, down the old street called the Tykesbrigge where the old German buildings stood, and then to the edge of the town, and by a winding upward path to one of Bergen's seven mountains. The mountain was wonderful. It was called Ulrikken. Little Ole liked to walk up this mountain, to imagine that he was a king, and that Ulrikken was his castle. How beautiful Bergen looked nestling by the blue fjord, and how strange and musical were the sounds of the wind that blew up here on the mountaintop, so much more strongly than in town.

Ole sat down in the grass by the side of a boulder. He emptied the small stones from his shoes. Then he looked around and stretched his legs out a bit. After a while, he picked up the violin, and, listening carefully to the wind, he tried to make the little fiddle reproduce its musical song.

It was shortly after this that Uncle Jens, who had also

23

set out to enjoy the fine day by walking on the mountain top, saw his nephew sitting in the grass and playing on the small fiddle. He was not surprised, as little Ole had always gone off on these long rambles.

"Hello, hello," he called.

Ole, intent upon the playing, did not hear.

Jens came up and sat down by the boy. "Well," he said, "you've come on a fine walk, and you're far from home. I think I'll sit down and listen to you play. Is that all right?"

Ole nodded. "I can make it sound like the wind," he said. He picked up the bow, and then with the utmost intentness, reproduced the soughing and crying of the wind.

Jens was greatly astonished. He looked at Ole. "Good, good," he said. "That really is wonderful."

"I can make it sound like birds too," said Ole calmly. He played some bird calls, and again accurately reproduced the sounds. When he saw his uncle's surprise and interest, he continued to play, smiling and laughing and talking to the little violin. "This is a waterfall," he said, "the big one that sounds like a drum."

He played a drumming sound. "It is the waterfall, isn't it?" he asked.

Jens exclaimed in delight. "Why, Ole, you are a whole orchestra. It is very good, indeed. You get the sounds of nature amazingly well."

As they talked together, Jens made suggestions, and Ole listened intently, and was able to put into practice almost at once, the improvements that his uncle suggested. The two spent a long time together on the mountain. There was the blue day, the music, and the interesting talk to keep them.

A few days after little Ole's ramble on the mountain Ulrikken, the family moved to the country for the summer. Johan Bull had a beautiful country place called Valestrand. Ole thought it was fairyland. It was on an island which was wild and wooded. There were many small streams that cascaded over rocks and stones in enchanting miniature rapids and whirlpools. There were ravines where mosses and ferns and white birches grew, and through which the streams came tumbling. But there was something else about the land, an odd and unusual feature, that was the cause of something very interesting that happened to Ole.

In the forests near Valestrand, there are certain sections where great rocks pile up. In these rocky sections, there are some odd rounded holes which are very large. Because of their round shape and smooth sides, they look like the inside of a giant's kettle. The people call these stone hollows "giants' cauldrons." They were made by glaciers many years ago, by the rolling and twisting of a large boulder. These giants' cauldrons, lying often in a shaded bower-like glen, always interested any children who saw them. It was so easy to imagine giants using them, stirring up a giant pudding or a giant porridge.

It did not take Ole long to find one of these cauldrons. It lay in a thickly wooded glen not far off the main road. It was smooth and round, about the size of a large bed, and was surrounded by delicate ferns and vines, and small wild flowers. When little Ole climbed into it, he thought it was like a fairy orchestra shell. The sloping sides of the glen and the thick stand of pines and birches made it private. At once, he recognized it as his particular place, made especially for him and the little yellow violin. He went to it secretly in the morning, or the late afternoon, and always, as he pushed into this secret glen, through all the tangle of greenery, he was excited to come again, and his heart beat so rapidly it seemed to take his breath away.

It was not long after this time that alarming rumors went, round the near-by town. The country people said that strange sounds and ghostlike music could be heard coming from the forest. Some told the old stories of hobgoblins, and trolls, and the giants that lived under the mountains. Early one morning, two Norwegian farmers were going down the forest road. They were driving their cattle up to the mountain dairy farm, and, as they came down the road, at the point nearest the glen, both stopped suddenly. "Did you hear something?" said one.

"I thought I did," answered the second.

"It must be the waterfall in the glen," said the first. But as he spoke, a look of fearful uncertainty came over his face. This time, there was no mistaking the sounds, queer, muffled, indistinct, like a kind of unearthly singing. After a few minutes the sounds stopped, and there was only the silence of the forest. The two men went on, more rapidly now, prodding the cattle to a faster walk.

That night in the village inn, someone else spoke of hearing weird music on the road near the glen, and a few days later three women came home badly frightened. "There are certainly trolls in the cauldrons," they said.

The men sitting around the inn laughed. "Such things are nonsense," they said.

But there were others present who had heard the sounds and who were more than ever puzzled. In a few days, there were so many rumors about ghosts, hobgoblins, and trolls, that the mountain people said the spirits of the mountains had come back to take possession of the valleys, and that the roads were no longer safe. The stories finally became so alarming that one of the men decided to investigate. He went to the glen at sunset, and as he came towards it, he heard music clearly. It was plaintive and sweet, like the voice of the forest. He followed the music through the forest and came finally to Ole's glen. And there he saw the little goblin. It was Ole sitting in the giants' cauldron, playing a weird march on his tiny violin.

The secret was out. When the farmer told the story in the village, there was much talk and laughter. "So, you are the goblin, Ole," the people said when they saw him.

At first Ole did not like it that his glen had been discovered, but after all it was a small tragedy. All of the forest called to him, and he soon had other favorite woodland walks where he went with his violin.

The good summer at Valestrand passed quickly for him. He liked to row on the fjords and to swim. He liked to listen to the stories that his grandmother told him, and to talk with the country people and hear the country legends that they had to tell. But more than anything else he always liked to play the violin. He did this as naturally and as easily as other boys talk or run. His violin playing, though not conventional or correct, had great persuasiveness and charm, and everyone who heard the little boy was carried away by his engaging personality and appealing music.

In time, he would have a great success with his music, and a career that would lead him to fascinating adventures.

27

CHAPTER 3

UNIVERSITY YEARS

So young Ole Bull grew up, living at Bergen and beautiful Valestrand. He always played the violin, and composed music of his own which was full of strange and poetic passages. He loved Norwegian scenes, and always, in his music, he tried to express the beauty and grandeur of his land. His education was never ordered and disciplined. He studied music briefly with a certain Herr Paulsen, a Dane, and again for a short time with a Herr Lundholm. But the time was not long, and Ole's father never encouraged the study. Nevertheless, Ole's desire drove him to play. He was always playing, and his natural gift was so lyrical and poetic and warm, and his personality so striking and winsome, that wherever he appeared, and whenever he played, it was as though there were a celebration.

When Ole Bull was seventeen, his father decided that he must go off to the University and submit to the university studies and disciplines. The University was at Oslo the capital of Norway, then called Christiania. So it was there to Oslo that the tall fair young Norseman made the first of his many journeys out into the world. Soon his life would be like a merry opera, full of people and surprising scenes.

On the night before Ole was to leave for the University, Johan Bull had a long talk with his son.

"As you know," he said, "it is my wish to see you become a pastor, the leader of a village. For a long time, I have tried to direct your studies to that end. I think you could be a success if you would put your mind to the study. You talk well, and with persuasiveness. People are attracted to you and have confidence in you. Your character is good. I think the work of a pastor is the noblest work of all. If only—" Johan Bull stood up, clasped his hands behind his back, and walked with nervous irritation over to the window. "If only," he went on, "you could keep your mind from the fiddling. As a pleasure, it is all very well, very refreshing, but a man must have solid work to do in the world."

"Yes, I know," Ole answered.

"Now, I want you to promise me this. Do not yield to your extreme desire for the violin. It will get you nowhere. Stick to work, and then later, after you are established, there will be time for the enjoyment of music."

The next day, Ole started off on one of the little Bergen boats. All of his family came down to see the beginning of his first journey out into the world. He climbed on board. In one hand he carried his heavy bag, and in the other, his violin in its case. He was excited, finding himself at last going off alone to begin his career. "This is the beginning," he thought, "the first of the good time that belongs to me."

He put down the bag, but kept the violin in his hands. He looked at the harbor filled with its forests of masts, the bright red-roofed town, the seven mountains and the harbor islands, and then, at last, at his brothers and sisters, his father and his mother. He felt strongly his love of Norway and of his family. It was like a fire smoking, or a wave pounding inside him. As he stood on the deck of the little boat, he looked extraordinarily handsome, tall, straight, vigorous, with strong shoulders developed by the years of rowing on the fjords.

The little boat backed slowly out into the water.

"Good-by," called Ole's mother, her eyes shining with pride at her handsome son.

"Good-by, remember your promise," called Johan Bull. "And good luck to you, my boy."

"Good-by," he answered. As the boat began to move, he waved at them all, smiling, and continuing to feel his great love for them.

The boat turned into the fjord, and the town and his family were almost immediately lost to Ole's view. He continued to stand, however, looking at the familiar green shores. Sometimes the water passageway was so narrow, and the rocky shores so close, that he could reach out and touch overhanging tree branches. The early spring vegetation was luxuriant and beautiful, and at many points Ole could see the deep blue anemones of spring and the wild white moonflowers. He knew all of this country well, the flowers, the grottos, and the little hidden ravines. After some time had passed, he opened the violin case and picked up his violin. Unconsciously he stroked it, as he had done as a small boy, and then placed it caressingly on his shoulder, and began to play.

At first the notes were clear and fairylike, like the tones of a fine silver bell. Then a capriciousness came into the music. At one moment there would be a fantastic whirl of melody, full of gaiety and wild leaping spirit. Then there would follow passages of weird melancholy, strangeness, tenderness, and disturbing dissonance. The notes carried clearly over the water. They echoed against the rocks and came flying back with such darting speed that they were like an accompaniment sung by the wild spirits of the caves and glens.

"It's Ole Bull," the passengers said.

"Ole Bull," whispered the children.

"Ole Bull," said the sailors.

They all listened intently and in silence, while the boat carried them slowly down the winding Bergen fjord. Ole played for about an hour, until the boat left the rocky walls of the fjord and turned out into the open sea.

Oslo, capital city of Norway! Oslo, city of crowds, and shops, and spacious avenues! Home of a young University, home of an orchestra! Center of ideas, of hot-headed student talk! There was a new air stirring in the old city. Ole Bull felt it as he walked down the principal street. There were the students, talking in the pastry shops, talking, talking as they walked the avenue.

"I have come to the right place," Ole Bull thought. "I was a seven-sleeper in Bergen, a mountain fiddler. I need to wake up, to study, and to make something of myself."

He set out briskly down the avenue, taking long strides and breathing the clear air, feeling strong, certain, directed in the way he would go. Yes, Oslo was delightful in its briskness and cleanness. It was not like Bergen, a town in a fairy tale. He stopped before the window of a bookshop.

Many books were spread out, more than he had seen in all the Bergen shops together. As he stood, someone came up behind him.

"Good evening," said a voice. "Shall we knock the window in? It would be a good thing. Look. Every title is in Danish. Every word is in Danish. Every thought and expression is Danish. And why should it not be Norwegian? Are we not Norwegians? Do not Norwegians have a language and thoughts and expressions as well as the Danes? Must we go and live with the trolls in the mountains to escape from these Danes?"

Ole turned and found himself looking into the face of a young man of his own age, as tall as himself, as large and as striking in appearance. This young man continued to talk with heat.

"I am Henrik Wergeland," he said, "a student at the University, and this is the largest bookshop in town. Every time I walk by and see the display, I want to kick the window in. But—I end tamely. I shout, 'To the trolls with it!' Then I go on and drink chocolate in the next pastry shop, talk with a few crackpots, and go home. But who are you? I have not seen you before."

Wergeland looked at Ole's height and broad shoulders. He laughed. "One could not easily miss you in a crowd."

Ole was attracted to Henrik Wergeland. He introduced himself, and said that he had come to be also a student at the University.

Wergeland listened with interested attention. "Come," he said at once. "We will have supper at a café. It is a little way down the street. The food is hearty, and good enough, and the fish is shipped in from Bergen."

When they went in, the café was packed full of students from the University. They were all talking, and there was so much noise that Wergeland had to shout to be heard. "There is a table at the back," he said.

The two pushed their way through the crowd, and found the table a little apart from the others. The waiter came at once and took Wergeland's order—herring for two, boiled potatoes, flatbrod, pastries, and sweet chocolate.

"My family also came from Bergen," shouted Henrik. "My grandfather lived there. People called him the 'turbulent head.' I am said to be like him, also a 'turbulent head.' "

"Well, what are you turbulent about?" Ole shouted back, laughing.

Wergeland instantly became serious. "Do you mean to say you do not know? And after our meeting in front of the bookshop? I am turbulent about everything. There is everything here to be turbulent about. I am always in a turmoil, like a storm. I am like a storm about our country, Norway. Norway, Norway, *Gamle Norge,* Mother Norway! Do you know our country has been free and independent of Denmark since 1814? It is now 1828. That is fourteen years. Yet we have no Norwegian writers, no Norwegian painters, no Norwegian musicians. We are docile. We follow the Danes. Let the trolls put them all in a pickle, I say! Let us kick in the windows so full of Danish books! Let us have talk in Norwegian, and writing in Norwegian, and music and art and politics in Norwegian!"

Wergeland relaxed for a moment as the waiter brought the plates of herring. He laughed and waved his arms. "You see," he said, "I am very turbulent, a 'turbulent

33

head' like my grandfather." He leaned on the table and looked directly at Ole. His whole personality was wonderfully winning, magnetic, and vigorous. He began to talk rapidly, sketching the facts of Norwegian history. He spoke of the four hundred years of Danish domination when the Danish capital, Copenhagen, was the center of Scandinavian culture.

"Copenhagen is a European city," he said. "Have you seen it? Well, no matter, you will soon enough. It is neat, well-ordered, worldly. There are theaters, museums, and an opera house. Many people there know the art of living. They know how to dress and dine well. There is good talk, communication. Edges are smoothed. They are people, not of one country, but of the world. But we Norwegians—we are provincial. We are country cousins. We are bears from the mountains. We are bashful, ill at ease, awkward, and clumsy."

Wergeland again stopped for a moment, and, seeing the sympathetic attitude of his new friend, shrugged his shoulders. "There is no need to go on and on like a storm. But everyone must help. It is important that we express the pride that we feel in our country. It is important to talk. Ideas come from talking. It is important for our dignity, and for the world that we cease to be country cousins."

Wergeland settled to his food and ate fish and potatoes with relish.

At this moment, a group of students came over to the table. One was from Bergen and had seen Ole Bull come into the cafe with Wergeland. "Hello," he said, his red face beaming with pleasure, "I heard you were coming." He turned to his friends. "This is Ole Bull, the violinist."

34

Ole jumped up and was introduced to the crowd. His smile, his air of genial dignity, combined with his striking height and assurance, made an immediate impression.

"You must play for us, Ole," shouted his friend. "We must hear your violin."

Ole Bull looked around the café. How was he not to play? How deny the violin bow in its case at his side? How deny the desire in his fingers and arm, and the excitement in his heart? How could the promise made to his father be kept, or even be remembered at a moment such as this?

The violin took charge and led Ole and the crowd in the café with it. It led certainly and magically, just as the Pied Piper had led away the village children in the fairy tale. And when Ole stopped, out of breath and smiling, still it was not the end, for the students shouted for more and more and more. At last, one pushed his way to the front of the crowd.

"Tonight," he said, "there is a concert for charity. You must play. We will take you to the hall. All the students and professors will be there."

But now, at the direct question, Ole remembered the promise given to his father. "No," he said, still out of breath, "my father has forbidden me to play for public concerts."

"But you cannot do that. Surely your father would not keep you from doing an act of charity."

"Well," said Ole doubtfully.

"Of course not, that is unthinkable."

So as it turned out the promise proved impossible to keep. Ole played that night, and the next, and most of the nights thereafter. He played alone, and with a quartet in the home of a University professor, and then with the Oslo orchestra. And always the music that came out like a burst of sunlight, full of wonderful runs, and quakes, and quavers, led and directed him like a powerful genie. He failed in his studies and examinations, giving all of his time to music.

In the fall, though he was only eighteen years old, he became the leader of the Oslo orchestra. He was immensely popular. Whenever he stepped on the concert platform, he brought with him an air of celebration. He was so young and tall, so full of health and beaming youthful spirit. Often the success and applause went to his head, and he liked to dazzle the audience with showy effects, storms of brilliant runs and arpeggios. Sometimes he settled down and knew that he ought to study music seriously with a strict and scholarly musician.

"I do not know harmony," he thought, "or the laws of composition. I cannot be certain of playing correctly the classic works." But he did not have the habit of work or study, and he did not subject himself to discipline. Yet there was seriousness in him, and the desire to reach the heights of musical accomplishment. Wergeland once said that he was like a balloon, straining and tugging to get loose into the upper air.

The two had many talks in the cafés and in Wergeland's rooms. Henrik Wergeland did more for Ole Bull than anyone whom Ole met in Oslo. This is not surprising, for Wergeland soon would become one of Norway's leaders, one of the strongest and boldest workers for independent Norway. Now, as a student, he talked ardently of his country. "Norway, Norway, *Gamle Norge!*" he was always exclaiming. He wrote long poems and articles about his country, and was one of the first to express the spirit of his small beautiful land.

"Ole," he said seriously one day, "you are what I dream of being. You do easily what I must work hard to do. You are like a fire. Everyone who hears you is kindled. You play our folk songs and mountain melodies, and by so doing, you light fires of patriotism, simply by your mood and your excitement. You compose a little, bagatelles, puffs of smoke with gleams of fire in them. But you must do much more. You have imagination and the gift of stirring imagination."

It was shortly after this talk with Wergeland that Ole Bull decided to leave Oslo. More than a year had passed since he had come to the capital city. He knew now there was only one way for him to go, the way that his violin would take him. He decided to go to Germany, to study seriously with a musician by the name of Spohr whom many considered greater than the master Beethoven. He set out on May 18. He was full of hope, and confidence, and the certainty of success. It seemed to him that he wanted this success not for himself only, but for his country, Mother Norway. Whenever he thought of his country, the mountain folk songs with their wild curious melodies came into his mind and stayed there. At such moments, the beauty of music and the beauty of his land were one and the same to him, and he wanted to play on and on without stopping, telling the world of Norway's grandeur, her mountains, and fjords, her deep and silent glens, and all the various islands that lay like jewels along the irregular coast. Such a land, he thought, could rightly be described only in music or in poetry.

CHAPTER 4

OLE BULL'S FIRST SUCCESS

What happened in Germany was a great pity. Sometimes a little thing, of such slight importance that afterwards one cannot even remember it, ruins an important moment. It may be merely an expression of the face, a tone of the voice, an awkward attitude, or a smile in the wrong place. So it would be with Ole Bull. He rejoiced when he came into Germany. One can imagine him, listening to the new language and enjoying the new scenes and the people. He had always liked picturesque places, and the old German cities with their narrow streets and gabled houses were full of the atmosphere of the olden times.

The monuments in the parks, the many schools and libraries, the ancient castles, and above all the feeling of a past, richer than anything like it in Norway, inspired respect in the young man from the land of mountains. As he came into the town of Kassel, where the musician Spohr lived, he particularly felt the charm of a fine European city. Kassel was very old, and the monuments and parks and avenues were handsome and distinguished. He sat down in one of the parks before a splashing fountain. The sounds of piano music came from an open window. The player was

38

skillful, and the clear notes gave an added quality to the charming scene.

"I will study hard with Spohr," Ole thought as he looked at the falling water. "I should have had teaching all of my life. My father was both right and wrong. Wrong in keeping me from my violin, but right in wanting me to study. Wergeland gave the reason for his feelings. We have no Norwegian arts, no contacts to show how high a value the world puts upon music and arts. But I think it's not too late for me to learn. Spohr is a great man. He will know what I must do."

Ole sat longer by the splashing fountain. He looked what he was, a young man from the north, handsome, tall, a little awkward, unused to the ways of a European city. He enjoyed greatly the scene before him, yet perhaps even this enjoyment was unfortunate for him. He stayed long by the fountain, and all of the time his thoughts were not like those familiar to Wergeland or his friends at home. They were not arrogant, but humble, of a searching seriousness, and they were mixed up with dreams of becoming one of the first violin talents of Europe.

In this quiet and receptive mood, Ole at last stood up. "I must go to Spohr," he thought, "the afternoon is half gone."

He made his way to the house and was admitted after only a few moments of waiting to see the famous man.

Spohr looked up and saw the tall young stranger. "Well, good day," he said, "what do you want?"

He spoke precisely, and without expression.

"I have come more than five hundred miles to hear you play, Herr Spohr," Ole said.

39

Spohr had taught all day, and he was to give a concert that evening in the village of Nordhausen, some miles away.

"I cannot play for all who ask," he answered. "If you want to hear me, go to Nordhausen. I am about to go to the music festival there to give a concert. And now, will you excuse me, there are things I must do."

He rose, bowed stiffly, and Ole knew nothing else to do but leave. He found himself again outside the house which he had studied with so much respect and interest a few moments before. The dreamed-of moment had come and had passed. As Ole walked away, the city of Kassel no longer looked charming to him. He kicked at some pebbles lying in the grass.

"The trolls take him and all the teachers!" he thought savagely. The receptive, seeking mood that he had had all during the afternoon which would have made Wergeland so greatly rejoice, went away, and he felt resentment, and anger, and coldness. He went alone to a café for supper, but he no longer enjoyed either the place or the food. Nevertheless, he did make the journey to Nordhausen to hear the master play; but enthusiasm destroyed would not come again easily to Ole Bull. Perhaps the unhappy afternoon determined his mood, because the music of Spohr seemed to him cold, without imagination, or color, or poetry.

"If that is fine music," he thought, "I will not be a musician."

When he left that night, he was angry and hurt, and more disappointed than he knew. What he had most counted upon was taken from him. Perhaps if he had gone to Spohr at another hour, or on another day when the musician was less busy, all might have been different. But the time passed, and Ole Bull would never again seek out a great teacher.

He stayed for a while in Germany, went wandering with a crowd of German students. They made merry, carousing, singing, playing, drinking, and eating heartily in the garden cafés. Ole was like a minstrel or a singing troubador. He won the crowds by his appearance, his genial manner, and his astonishing performance on his violin. He enjoyed the life. It was hearty and boisterous like a merry opera, full of travel, people, adventure, and music.

After Germany and a visit home, he went to Paris and lived there for almost two years. He heard good music at the great opera house in Paris, and he made interesting friends. One was a Pole, young Frederic Chopin, and the two liked to go exploring in the many book and music shops of Paris. Ole felt the stimulation and great charm of Paris, but he was not trained to have any success there. The opera house did not open its doors to one who was unknown, to one not recommended by a famous teacher. So finally, after ups and downs, good days and bad ones, Ole left Paris and went to Italy. It was there, in the musical southern land, that he had the surprising adventure that led him to fame and fortune. It happened in this way.

By chance he went first to the city of Bologna. He came into Bologna at night and took an upper room in a shabby hotel which he thought was suitable for his purposes. It was quiet, and away from the main streets of the city.

"I can be alone here with my violin," he thought. "I will write a concerto. I can have silence. There is a good inn around the corner where I can breakfast and dine. When I grow tired, I can explore the streets. In the daytime, I can soak up some of the good Italian sunshine. Perhaps—who can tell?—something may come of the concerto."

The first few days passed as Ole had planned. Each day he worked on his music, dined, walked, and returned later in the evening to his room. Then before going to bed, he would take his violin and play, sometimes the new composition, but more often the plaintive folk songs of Norway. He also began to try the folk songs of Italy which were also full of melody, yet sweeter, gayer, simpler, uncomplicated by northern moodiness and northern melancholy.

When Ole Bull played, it was as it had always been since the days of childhood. He played on and on, going from one mood into another. And as the time passed, and the wonderful songs flowed from his open window, the street below filled with Italians. They stood together in the dark listening. "It is the voice of an angel," one man whispered.

"No, it is the stranger, the tall young man who has taken the garret room. He plays on a big violin."

"Can that be possible! What a singing tone! Like a poem, so beautiful, so sad!"

Now it happened that in Bologna at this time, there was a famous orchestra. Its leader, Signor Zampiere, had engaged as soloist one of the most famous operatic stars of the day, a Madame Malibran. This Madame Malibran was brilliant, but temperamental, and one night just before a concert, because of some fancied insult, she sent word to the director that she would not appear. Zampiere stared at Madame Malibran's messenger. He sputtered and turned red in the face.

"But that is impossible!" he shouted. "The audience is already coming into the theater. She must appear."

The messenger shrugged and turned up his hands. "Signor, Madame Malibran said that the appearance was not possible for her tonight."

At this difficult moment, a Madame Rossini, a fine artist and musician who was present at the scene, touched Zampiere's arm.

"I have a suggestion, signor," she said, "and I beg you to believe what I have to say. A few nights ago as I was driving home from the late evening concert, I heard music that was like nothing I have ever known. I stopped to listen. It was coming from the open window of a shabby inn. There was a crowd below the window in spite of the lateness of the hour and the darkness. All were listening in the most complete silence to the music. It was a violin, signor, and truly it was a divine one. I determined then to go and tell you. I can take you to the place. It is not far from here. If you could find the player, I am certain he would be a substitute for Madame Malibran."

Zampiere stared in astonishment at Madame Rossini. "What madness is this!" he exclaimed. "A stranger! One completely unknown! You're not making this suggestion seriously?" Then Zampiere paused. He could hear the audience in the theater. Of course, such a proposal as that of Madame Rossini was impossible, but what was he to do? He looked at her again and saw that she was serious. He knew well her sound knowledge of music and the excellence of her musical taste.

"Be quick," he said at last. "Let us go and find him."

He caught up his hat. The two ran outside, jumped into

43

a carriage, and Madame Rossini directed the way to the inn where she had heard the music.

Now it happened that on this particular night, Ole Bull had gone to bed early. He had spent the day walking in the country, and, coming home, overcome with weariness, had gone to sleep. But now, there was a rain of knocks on his door, and a voice shouting: "Wake up, wake up, young man! *Cospetto di Bacco*, what stairs!"

Ole did not wake at once, but in a few minutes as the knocks and shouts continued, he got up and opened the door. To his great astonishment, he saw a fat Italian in evening dress, red-faced, and out of breath from the stairs. Without explaining who he was, Zampiere continued to shout: "Hurry, hurry, young man. There is no time to be lost. Play for me. I must hear you at once."

Ole thought he was dreaming. What was this stranger talking about? Why was he here? But Zampiere was shouting again. "Play for me, young man. Improvise. Let me hear you at once!"

In a daze Ole began to play. After he had played a few bars, Zampiere stopped him. "Let Malibran have her headache," he said. "Come with me, young man. You are to play for my concert."

Ole dressed quickly while Zampiere explained what had happened, and the three hurried back to the concert hall. When Ole saw the distinguished audience and the stage lights, it was as though he had been brought by magic to the scene.

Zampiere pushed him out on the stage. "Choose your own composition," he whispered.

Ole stood for a moment before the lights and the peo-

44

ple, and then, still feeling as though it must all be a dream, he began to play. He began softly, with a tender dreaminess and melancholy. In a few minutes he had cast a spell over the sentimental Italians. He led them on through a maze of tender passages. As the minutes passed and Ole felt the sympathy of his audience, he began to be exhilarated. The surprise of this success, its oddness and charm, went to his head. The violin now took charge, and Ole's bow began to fly over the strings with abandon and fire. The fast-flying arpeggios came out in a burst of swiftness and brilliance. Whereas a few moments before, the Italians had been melting with tenderness, now they were electrified. When Ole finished, they stood up to shout and applaud.

"Bravo, bravo!" they called out in their enthusiasm.

Ole smiled and bowed and stepped forward to acknowledge the shouts. After that, he played again and again. When the director thought that his strength must be at an end and would have stopped him, Ole stepped forward once more. "I will play! Oh, you must let me play," he said, his face glowing with the work and with the first success which had come to him so strangely in the night.

There was unrestrained enthusiasm when he at last finished the concert, and so many flowers were thrown on the stage that for a few moments it was as though he were standing in a rain of flowers.

"Ah, young man," said Zampiere when they were finally off the stage and away from the crowd, "never have I heard such playing. Come now. Tell me about yourself. Who are you? Why are you hiding yourself away at the top of all those devilish stairs?"

45

But before Ole could answer, there was a clatter at the door, and a crowd of Italians burst in. "We will escort the artist home!" they shouted. "Where is he? Let us see him."

And after Ole had laughed and bowed and showed them the big violin, they unhorsed the carriage that he had come in, and pulled it through the streets, singing and shouting for him. Ole could not understand Italian, and the Italians of course knew no Norwegian, but they all understood each other because the language of laughter and friendliness and emotion is the same for all people.

Ole stayed for two years in Italy, and all of the time was good for him. The enthusiasm of the Italians inspired him, and he became confident and certain of his powers. He spent the hot summer in the Italian mountains and loved the peaks and valleys because they reminded him of Norway.

He had success also with his composing. There were two compositions of this time that later became famous when he played them in concert halls all over Europe and the United States. One was called *The Mother's Prayer*. This was a plaintive appealing melody. It came to him one morning, the violin seeming to sing the notes. Later, when the piece was famous, he liked to tell how it came to him. These are his words:

"I had been up all night with the moon, sympathizing with her. I had thought of Norway, of home, of many sad things. I took my violin, and it sang to me so sweetly the thoughts of the night! I wrote down its voice, and as this brought before me the image of a mother kneeling at the altar, entreating for her child, I called it *The Mother's Prayer*."

46

The second piece composed at this time was even more famous. It is called *Polacca Guerriera.* The story of its composition is very interesting. Ole had gone at midnight to see the famous Italian volcano, Mount Vesuvius. The loneliness of the hour, the huge form of the mountain, the fire spurting up into the sky and falling back in a cascade of flame, the lordly smoke clouds—all combined to make a deep impression upon him. As he stood entranced, music began to come to him, fast, mysterious, leaping music, disturbing and fascinating, like fire.

He wrote down this music later in Rome and played it for a concert there. The effect was even greater than he had imagined. The sharp brilliant theme took the excitable Italians by surprise. The soaring singing melody, played in powerful strokes, affected them in the same way that the rain of Vesuvius' fire had affected Ole. At the end of the composition, the violin carries four distinct parts, and there is a continuous shake for fifteen bars. This shake was like electricity to the Italians. Ole performed it superbly, his imperial bow moving with lightning swiftness, and pouring out sparkling notes like a rain of fire. When he finished, the applause was like a tempest. Ole bowed again and again. His princely appearance, his erect carriage, slim waist, well-developed shoulders, and smiling youthful dignity appealed to the Italians. He looked to them like a young Apollo.

After these Italian concerts, the name and fame of the Norwegian violinist spread like the wind. He played at Florence under the patronage of a famous prince. He played at Lucca for the Queen Dowager herself. At Naples, the fair city of song and melody, he had a great triumph. A

47

critic there wrote: "What sorcery must a violin possess to electrify the Neapolitans!"

When Ole left Italy to go to Paris, he was no longer the obscure violinist from the northland. The Paris Opera House, one of the great and distinguished operas of the world, invited him to appear as a solo performer. He played his *Polacca* there to the tremendous audience, and the applause was like thunder. In the newspapers of Paris, on the day following the concert, the critics were full of enthusiasm. One wrote of Ole's "boldness, his spirit, the wonderful speed of his bow, the purity of his tone, the depth of his feeling." Another wrote that his playing was "full of soul and energy, of mysticism and charm; his violin sang with so much expression that one could almost believe that it was a human voice."

So Paris was conquered as well as Italy.

It was heady, wonderful, and stimulating for Ole. What was yet more wonderful, was that Ole's success was more important than the usual success of one man. It gave his country, the *Gamle Norge* he was always talking about with so much affection, her first famous man. It gave the people who hoped for Norway's arts pride and encouragement, and a proof that success was possible for them.

Ole gave this gift to his country, and soon, because of his fame and success and the stimulation he was always able to give, he would be able to do much more. The time of his great contribution was almost at hand.

CHAPTER 5

AMERICA

To London, Spain, Germany, Russia went the minstrel of
the North. He traveled in a great English carriage, large
enough for him and a servant to sleep in. In the winter it
was equipped with runners. Eight horses pulled it through
the snows, and Ole slept under a mound of bearskins.
Everywhere the people flocked to his concerts, attracted by
his music and by his personality, which made everything
that he did take on a festive air.

In England, the Duke of Devonshire gave him a cluster of diamonds which Ole had set in the tip of his violin
bow.

In Spain, the young Queen Isabella fell in love with
the handsome Norwegian. She offered him a generalship
in the Spanish army which he declined, and, upon his leaving, gave him a pin in the shape of a verbena, set with one
hundred and forty diamonds.

In Russia, he played in the Imperial Theater in St.
Petersburg. His *Polacca Guerriera* created the greatest
enthusiasm, and when he concluded by playing the national anthem, there was another furor. The Empress gave

him a vast emerald in a setting of over a hundred diamonds.

After all the adventures in Europe, Ole decided that he must see the United States, the new world, where, according to all the reports, a famous artist of Europe could have a great success. He made his plans happily and set out in the autumn.

In November, 1843, the New York *Herald* printed this announcement: "Ole Bull, the prince of violinists, from Europe, is expected here tomorrow by the steamer. He is the greatest and best of the lot in the old world, is a fine looking young man, and fights like a tiger."

Ole took rooms at the old Astor House. He had many callers who had heard the stories about him, and he delighted them all by his courtly manners, his interesting odd way of speaking English, and by his enthusiasm for the new world. His first concert was one of the great nights for the New York stage. It took place in the Park Theater, and the scene was brilliant. The decorations on the walls were crimson and gold. Huge chandeliers of myriad small gaslights gave a flickering softened light. A large portrait of Shakespeare gazed down upon the audience from above the arch of the stage, and as for the audience, it was fully as interesting to see. The ladies wore their hair in long curls, and their dresses were full and billowing over hoop skirts. The gentlemen were very dignified and wore great cravats and flapping collars.

Ole played his *Polacca Guerriera,* and the showy piece, with the continuous shake at the end lasting for fifteen bars, dazzled this New York audience just as it had the Italians at its first playing. The newspapers the next day were full of reports of the concert. The *Herald* said:

"We cannot describe Ole Bull's playing. It is beyond the power of language. Some of his unearthly, his heavenly, passages work on the feelings and the heart till the very tears flow. At the close of some of his wonderful cadences, the very musicians in the orchestra flung down their instruments and stamped and applauded like madmen."

After this first New York concert which was such a success, Ole gave six more concerts in New York during one month, and each one was a triumph for him. Then he began a tour of the United States which took him into nearly every city east of the Mississippi. The adventures that he had on this tour would fill a book. The traveling conditions in the West were poor. When winter came, Ole took along a huge buffalo coat and woolen socks to wear outside his boots. He usually carried pistols for protection against bandits, and as for means of travel, it was both difficult and complicated. The journey from New York to New Orleans took twelve days, and one had to travel by rail, by coach, by steamboat, and by canal boat. When the boats passed under the low bridges, the passengers often had to lie prone.

Ole enjoyed all the uncertainties, the rough and tumble life of the new, fast-developing country. He liked the river boats, the traveling coaches, and all the people that he met. He understood them, and they in turn understood him and liked his bigness and heartiness and zestful enjoyment of experiences. His European friends would have been surprised at some of these experiences.

Once, in a small town of the Southwest, Ole sat alone

with his violin case at his side in a dimly-lighted café. A rough-looking character came through the swinging door and approached Ole. He drew out a bowie knife and pointed it directly at the violinist.

"Give me the diamonds from your violin bow," he demanded.

Ole looked at the man steadily. "No," he said, "they cannot be given away. They are prized possessions of mine."

"I will have them anyway," the man said.

Ole got to his feet slowly. "All right," he said, "since I can do nothing else."

He stepped toward the violin case, but then in a quick movement, he turned and knocked the man sprawling on the floor. The knife left the hand of the would-be robber, and Ole quickly recovered it.

The man rose slowly to his feet and looked at Ole. They stood for a moment regarding each other. Then Ole held out the knife. "You made a mistake, my friend," he said. "Let us sit down and forget it."

The man agreed, but to the surprise of Ole, he would not take back the bowie knife. "It is yours," he said, "take it. I didn't think a fiddler could be so strong."

Ole accepted the knife, and in the years later, he had it in a case in his house in Norway. He enjoyed showing it to friends and telling its story.

On another occasion, on a Mississippi river boat, Ole was sitting peacefully in the sun enjoying the newspaper of a southeast frontier town. A man separated himself from a noisy group of frontiersmen. He came over to Ole and held out a flask of whiskey.

"Here," he said, "take a drink."

"Thank you," Ole answered, "but I cannot take whiskey. It is like poison to me."

The man grew angry. He looked at Ole for a minute, then shouted, "Well, if you can't drink, come on, fight then."

At once his companions crowded around, ready for the excitement. They joined the shouting. "Yes, if you can't drink, let's see how you can fight." They were a strange-appearing crowd in the rough and garish clothes of the frontier. "Come on, show us what you're good for," they shouted.

Ole stood up. "My friends," he said. "I am a Norseman from Norway. A Norseman can fight as well as anybody when his blood is up, but I can't fight when my blood is cold, and why should I?"

They all laughed. "So, the ge-entleman can fight, but he won't!" they jeered.

The first man to address Ole then went close to him. "What are you scared of?" he shouted. "You look like a strong fellow."

Then Ole, seeing how things were, quietly said: "I will tell you what I will do. Let any one of you take hold of me in anyway he likes, and I'll wager that in half a minute he shall lie on his back at my feet."

A big fellow stepped forward, grinning. He would show Ole. The others stepped back, making a circle around the two. The big fellow grasped Ole around the waist. In one wrench Ole sent him sprawling on the deck. The men stared in astonishment. Several pulled out bowie knives, but, to the great relief of Ole, they used them to pry open

53

their flasks. The man on the deck was senseless, but after the contents of one of the flasks had been forced between his lips, he sat up. "How did I get here?" he roared.

His friends answered him with shouts of laughter. He got up, rubbed his head, and walked slowly around Ole. "Well," he said, "I reckon you're as quick as lightning."

Ole and the frontiersmen began to talk, and when they learned that he was a fiddler, they were more surprised than ever. In the next town, when Ole played, some of them came to the concert. It was in a dim hall, poorly lighted by smoking oil lamps. The men, however, sat quietly against the wall, chewing and smoking, and rocking in their chairs. The next day, Ole heard once again from the man he had knocked down. The editor of the town's newspaper had not sufficiently praised Ole's playing, and the man had gone to the newspaper office, loudly demanding to see the editor. He shook the paper in his face.

"This is no way to write about Ole Bull!" he yelled. "He's the strongest fiddler in the world!"

The astonished and frightened editor quickly promised to do better by Ole, and the incident came to a peaceful end.

When Ole heard the story later, he laughed heartily. "My fiddle and I have good friends," he said. "Sometimes we make them by music, and sometimes—well, perhaps the method must suit the circumstances."

Ole left the interesting frontier land of the United States. He went to Cuba to play and was delighted with the "fairylike" climate and the wonderful feeling for melody and rhythm that the Cubans possessed. From Cuba, he went up the coast of the United States and played in

Charleston, and Norfolk, and Baltimore. He went to Boston and visited there the poet, Longfellow, who became a lifelong friend. Ole was like a character in a book to Longfellow, and later the poet put him in one of his long poems. Ole is the fiddler in *Tales of a Wayside Inn*. Mrs. Longfellow was just as much delighted with Ole as was her husband. After his first Boston concert, she wrote in her diary: "A vast crowd, and vast applause. Saw returning home a dozen moons instead of one, intoxicated by this music."

Shortly after the visit with the Longfellow family, Ole's time in the United States came to an end. It had all been so interesting to him with all the kinds of experience that even as he sailed away he knew he would come back again and again. Of course he did not know that by the end of his life, the United States would be like a second home to him.

CHAPTER 6

A RARE VIOLIN

Of all of Ole Bull's many interests, perhaps the one closest to his heart after his playing, was the collecting of rare violins. He had had this interest from childhood, and as he acquired the money to do as he wished, he rarely could resist a fine instrument. He came to have a choice collection of instruments, and each had its own interesting story. One of these stories is particularly interesting, both because of the unusual circumstances by which the violin came to him, and more because of the quality of the instrument itself. It happened in this way:

In the city of Vienna in Austria, there lived a rich Bohemian who had a collection of musical instruments and violins that was the envy of all Europe. Among the violins was one which was beautiful in all ways, tone, and form, and ornamentation. The richest men of Poland, England, and Russia, had all tried to buy this violin, but its owner always answered to all offers, "No, not for the price of half Vienna."

What made the violin so wonderful was first of all its appearance. At its head was a beautifully carved and colored angel's face. Next to the little angel was a lovely mermaid also beautifully carved and colored. The mermaid's tail was covered with scales in green and real gold, and below her, all down the neck of the violin, were swirling designs in blue, red, and gold, like sunset light on the water of the sea. Just beneath the bridge of the violin, there was a second mermaid, this one all gold, and there were also two beautiful intertwining fishes. But the most wonderful thing of all about the violin was that its soft and singing tone was in harmony with its great beauty. When it was played upon by a master, one could imagine the angel and the mermaids singing strange and quiet harmonies. The artist who carved and painted all of this beauty was an Italian of the Middle Ages, called Cellini, and the maker of the violin itself was also an Italian, Da Salo.

It happened that when Ole Bull came to play his concerts in Vienna, the owner of the violin was in the audience. As soon as he saw Ole Bull step out on the concert platform and heard him play with all of his usual poetry and warm melody, the Bohemian decided that he would ask him to come and see his collections, and in particular, the rare violin. The two went to the Bohemian's palace together about midnight, after the concert. The palace was a rare place, the fitting home of a collection as rich and valuable as jewels.

"Come in," said the Bohemian, excitement in his voice. "I have many things here, not only violins."

A servant had gone in before them and lighted numerous candles. The room, which was high and vast, appeared to Bull like a sumptuous chamber in some Arabian Night's castle. The candle flames fell upon the polished surfaces of many a fine old instrument, piano and harpsichord, and organ. There was a wall of violins, and Ole Bull, who had always studied them and sought them out whenever he went on his travels, was entranced. He picked up one after another. The Bohemian pointed out a dark instrument.

"That one is rare," he said. "It is made of wood grown on the Italian side of the Alps. It is odd that the sunniness of Italy lives in Italian trees, and that instruments made from such wood give out a rich and mellow sound."

"I do not think it is strange," Ole Bull answered, "when even the kind of varnish used in the finishing makes so much difference, and when the age of the wood alone makes a difference in tone that is as great as day and night."

"If you are in love with old woods, look at this beauty," said the Bohemian. "This is my treasure." He took Ole now to the jewel of his collection, the ornamented Italian violin. He lifted it up and placed it in the hands of his guest. In the candlelight, the rich and fantastic carvings were extraordinarily beautiful. The whole instrument was like a medieval jewel.

Ole stared at it, turning it over and over, as fascinated as he had been when, as a child, Uncle Jens had given him the tiny yellow instrument, the first that he had ever owned.

"It is princely," he said at last. "I want it more than any instrument that I have ever seen. It has never been played, I think. There are no marks inside. My violins are scrolled on the inside with spirals and circles, the vibrations of my playing. How I should like to be the one to give the song of this one to the world!"

The Bohemian looked up at the stately figure of Ole Bull. "I would not part with it," he said. "But since tonight, since I have heard your playing, I will say this to you, Ole

Bull. If ever I have to part with it, on that day, I shall send word to you."

When the two friends parted at dawn, the Bohemian repeated his promise to Ole Bull in regard to the rare violin.

About two years passed. Ole Bull added other fine violins to his collection, some of them works of art, choice in the quality of tone, and in the beauty of their design. He did not hear further from the Bohemian, and put out of his mind the thought of owning the old Italian instrument. Then, one night, after a concert in Germany, he was dining with two famous musicians, Liszt and Mendelssohn. As the three talked, a servant came with a large envelope fastened with a heavy seal. Ole Bull pushed the envelope aside to open later, but Liszt protested.

"Open your letter, Ole Bull. It may be important," he said.

"I think not," Ole answered. "At least it is nothing that cannot wait."

"The seal is curious," said Liszt. "The design is familiar, but not clear."

Ole picked up the letter then, and opening it found that it was from the son of his friend, the Bohemian. The old man had just died, and in his will, there were orders that when the violin was offered for sale, it must be offered first to the minstrel of the North, Ole Bull.

"Yes," said Ole with excitement, "the letter is both important and very interesting." Then he began to tell of the evening when he had visited the palace of the Bohemian in Vienna and had seen the rare instruments shining in the candlelight.

Both Liszt and Mendelssohn were delighted with the

story. "If it comes to you," Liszt said at last, "let us dedicate it by playing together a sonata of the great Beethoven."

It was some weeks before Ole Bull received the violin. It was as beautiful as he remembered, and when he had it put in order ready for playing, he and Liszt and Mendelssohn dedicated it as they had planned, by playing the *Kreutzer Sonata* of Beethoven. One can imagine the scene, Liszt, tall as Ole Bull, with his shoulder-length hair, playing with a dazzling brilliance; Mendelssohn, letting fly swift and sparkling notes; and Ole standing erect, holding the violin lovingly, bringing out the winging notes from the wood that had grown in the Italian Alps. At last, after so many years, three famous musicians were giving singing voices to the angel and to the green and gold mermaids that had been carved and colored by the Italian artist, Cellini.

CHAPTER 7

NORWAY'S NATIONAL THEATER

After all the traveling, Ole Bull came home to Norway. This time his head was more filled with dreams than ever before. He had seen the wide world, people, and fine cities, and brilliant theaters, and he wanted more than anything now to start a Norwegian theater for the people. The words of Wergeland came often to his mind: "We must have Norwegian writers, Norwegian actors, Norwegian artists. Each country must express its own genius."

On his first night back in Bergen, after a good supper with friends at the inn, Ole Bull sat alone in the rooms that he had taken. He turned smiling towards his concert violin. "Oh, my poor fiddle," he said, "we are to work hard, you and I. Many concerts one after another, both to get money, and to stir up the people. Then we will build a theater for Norway. That will be fine, hi, fiddle?"

At this moment there was a knock at the door, and Madame Stork, who was the mistress of the house, came in.

"Oh, dear sir," she said, "dear Ole Bull, look out of the window. There is a sea of people shouting that they must see you. I told them you had arrived just this evening, but it made no difference to them, sir. They have heard of the bow with all the diamonds, and the diamond flower given by the Queen of Spain, and they want to see you and all the wonders, sir."

Madame Stork stopped talking, out of breath.

Ole Bull jumped up from his chair, and going to the window, he threw it wide open. The square before the house was packed with men, women and children. When they saw him, beaming down at them, they gave three hearty cheers. "Long live Ole Bull! Long live Bergen! Long live Norway!"

An old man in the crowd shouted: "Let us hear your violin, dear Ole. Let us see the diamond bow."

What could Ole do then but take out the big fiddle? He stood in the window and played the *Mountains of Norway*, and the *Saeter Girl's Sunday*. The sweet plaintive melody filled the square and went echoing against the walls of the old gabled houses, and floating off in the evening air toward the seven moutains. After the music, Ole Bull raised his hand for silence and began to talk. He talked as well as he played, with a natural spontaneity and warmth. He spoke of old Bergen, the loveliest town in the world, of Norway and its people who must take a place in the world with arts of their own. "Soon, I shall start a theater," he said, "and that will be only the beginning."

When the crowd went home after the talk, they were all ready to help with the wonderful new theater. They all saw their town through Ole's eyes, a lovely city full of old and fascinating things, gifted lavishly by nature with the sparkling sea, the fairylike islets, and the seven mountains. Indeed, it was fitting that in such a city, a national theater for Norway should have its start.

A few days later, there was an advertisement in the Bergen paper.

NOTICE

NORWEGIAN THEATER IN BERGEN

Men and women who want to make singing, music, acting, or national dancing their profession may now have engagements. Address yourself in writing as soon as possible to the National Theater in Bergen.

OLE BULL

Soon the people came crowding. Fiddlers from the mountains, dancers, peasant girls and peasant boys with bright cheeks and shining eyes, old men who had read the plays of Holberg and who wanted to speak the good, humorous lines; ladies who fancied themselves dressed up in velvets and feathers. Some of these people had talent, and some, of course, had no talent at all and could not even read. Some painters turned up, young men who wished to make stage scenery, and who had had no chance in Norway before. One young man was struggling desperately to write plays and to get them before an audience. He later became famous all over the world and his plays were produced in all the great cities. His name was Henrik Ibsen. He came to Ole Bull's theater, and because of it, was able to make his start at playwrighting.

But the first days were like a madhouse. It seemed to Ole and to those who helped him, that everyone in the city and in the valleys beyond wished to act or play in the theater. As if they did not make trouble enough, there was the problem of the theater building. It was fifty years old, in bad repair. The walls were black and stained, and there were no stoves to heat it in the cold of the Bergen winter.

"We will begin by making it cheerful," Ole Bull shouted to the group of workmen gathered in the old building. "We will paint it red. That will give the girls color, you know." After the painting was done, a shed was built around the front entrance so that each time the door was opened, at least the cold blasts could not drive in.

The days passed, and Ole and his helpers worked. The actors were weeded out, the musicians learned to follow Ole Bull's magic violin, and the building gleamed fresh and bright with all the red paint. August, September, October, November passed before the first performance could be given.

But the great night came at last, and Norway's first National Theater opened its doors. The audience was a mixed one. There were the people who believed in Ole Bull so fervently that they thought he could do anything, no matter how difficult. But there were others, the more sober people of the town who thought it would have been better to begin with a dramatic school, and to work up slowly to the great plan of a national theater.

One can imagine Ole Bull before the first performance. He had played before most of the kings and queens of Europe, and had appeared in most of the rich and handsome concert halls of the world, yet never had an evening's success seemed to him so important. On the morning of the great day, he had received a letter from a Norwegian poet. There were these lines in it:

"Norse Ole! My naive address will almost shock you, but I could find no title for you, and so far as I know the peasants call you only Ole Bull. Therefore Norse Ole may all go well!"

Ole Bull read and reread the letter. "Yes," he thought, "may all go well for me tonight because I am a Norseman, and great things for my country may come out of this undertaking."

In the red hall the people sat. They came warmly dressed, bundled up against the winter cold. When Ole Bull stepped out on the platform, he was surprised to see all the coats and mufflers and caps. He smiled, and there was a burst of hearty applause as he stepped up to the conductor's desk. Then the overture rang out, loud, full, and strong, as though each of the musicians felt Ole's confidence and spirit. Ole had never felt more inspired. He stood erect and handsome, and conducted with so much style, with such bold and dashing certainty that everyone in the audience sat up as though there were electricity in the air. After the overture, there came the play. It was an old play by the great Holberg who had lived two hundred years before in Bergen.

When the curtain came down, the actors behind the scenes danced and threw their arms around each other as they listened to the wild cheering of the audience. None had imagined such a success. At the height of all the enthusiasm, Ole Bull went out on the stage again with his violin in his hand. Lifting the large bow with the cluster of diamonds in the end, and accompanied by the inspired orchestra, he began his *Saeter Girl* melody. This song had almost become the official anthem of the town, and now its familiar haunting sweetness seemed to the people to give the evening its fitting climax and end. The intensely Norwegian quality of the music called up for the people typically Norwegian pictures of the lonely saeters and mountains. It strengthened the impressions of the evening, gave them a unity, and brought home Ole Bull's great idea, a theater that could express the genius of the Norwegian people.

When it was all over, there was a little feast in the theater for the actors and musicians. There were toasts and some fine speeches about the glorious future of Norwegian art. Perhaps the speeches were extravagant, but who would blame the speakers for that? Such a night of success would go to the heads of players with much more experience than the first actors of Norway's National Theater. The comedian in the play, a boisterous young man of nineteen years who was called Johannes Brun, took a piece of chalk, and on the door of the theater drew first a big nose. In front of the nose, he drew two hands spread out. This was young Johannes' way of thumbing his nose at the people who did not believe it was possible to make actors and musicians of the young people of Bergen.

Of course all of the nights were not like this first night of success. There were many odd problems to be solved. As the days passed, and the audience became more used to the theater, they made themselves more and more comfortable. They brought so many paper bags filled with sausage and huge pieces of bread that the actors had to shout to be heard above the rattling and munching. As the winter grew colder, the people came wrapped to the ears in scarves, layers of petticoats, furs, great coats. Ole Bull did

Ole Bull playing in his Norwegian mountain home.

not like this wadded appearance of the audience. At first he could do nothing about it, but finally he was able to have stoves put in the theater. However, the people were used to sitting in their outdoor clothes, and so at first did not remove them. One night, Ole determined to improve the appearance of the audience. He had blazing fires built in all of the stoves, and had young men ready to keep building them up as the flames died down.

"I will get the coats off," he said.

The room grew hotter and hotter. Finally it was unbearably hot. Some of the people began to take off their coats, but there were many who sat red-faced, making no sign of removing the thick wraps. The young men continued to put wood on the fires. Some of the people managed to hold out to the end, but by the end of the evening, most of them gave up and began to peel off their coats. Many weird costumes now came to light, as some of the women had not bothered to put skirts on over their colored petticoats. But after that evening, the appearance of the audience began to improve slowly.

The theater grew. Many people learned plays and music. Some learned social customs, as they needed to do in both dress and behavior. Most important of all, as Ole Bull had dreamed, pride in Norway grew, interest in the painting, and writing, and music of her people. All of these things strengthened the young artists and pushed them forward in their dreaming.

Ole Bull left the theater after it was well started. His work was the stirring up of enthusiasm for the starting. He had never had the gift of continuous, hard, and steady work, but he made his great and necessary contribution.

When he turned over the work to others, a young journalist wrote him this letter. It expressed the thoughts and feelings of most of the students of Norway.

"It is really astounding what an influence you have had on so many young people here. You have awakened an inner life and feeling in them. You are the spirit which brings thunder and flame, you open the way for us when we talk and work for Norway; but therefore you must never go away for too long at a time, for however eager and enduring we are, it is always done for the sake of Ole Bull. Do not forget that."

The years passed. To the end of his life, Ole was a great man of Norway, carrying abroad the name of his small country. He had a long life full of adventure, but his importance for Norway was best expressed by the young journalist in his letter at the time of the founding of the national theater. His sweet and haunting music, his striking personality, above all his fervent love for his mountain land, could not fail to impress all who saw and heard him. Then also, his liking for picturesque action and place constantly led him to play a part, to make a grand scene. People everywhere enjoyed these dramatic actions of Ole Bull, and talked yet more of the violinist from the Northland.

Once when he breakfasted with the royal family, the King of Norway made a playful suggestion. Ole had just played for the king his famous composition, *Saeterbesog*. The plaintive, bold melody rang through the room. The King looked at Ole. "You are going on a tour to Egypt,

Ole," he said. "You must play this northern melody on the top of the Cheops Pyramid."

The King smiled, but the suggestion appealed to Ole's love of the picturesque. When he came into Cairo, several months later, he decided to carry out the "royal idea," as he called it. Early on a February morning, he drove out to the Pyramid, taking with him a party of friends. He climbed the Great Pyramid, and then, taking his violin from a Bedouin who had carried it up for him, he lifted it in his arms. With powerful strokes, he played the best-loved melody of the Northland. The scene was strange but nevertheless interesting. The melancholy, strong, and appealing melody went out over the Nile and the desert, and the Egyptian city of minarets at the foot of the pyramid. When Ole had finished, the desert people rose and shouted, "Allah! Allah!"

Ole was elated at the romantic scene. Later he sent a telegram to King Oscar. "I played my *Saeterbesog* on the top of the Cheops Pyramid in honor of Norway and its beloved king."

Ole lived to be seventy, and all of the last years of his life were good. When he appeared anywhere, he made the occasion like a festival. He was white-haired, erect, and stately, and his manners were as courtly as ever. When he met a lady in the street, he would remove his top hat with a sweeping gesture and make a deep bow from the waist. Even when he said good-by on the telephone, he bowed toward the black box on the wall. One of his best friends was the American poet, Longfellow. When Ole Bull lived in Cambridge, Massachusetts, during some of the winters, the two were often together. The people of the town enjoyed watching them. Each was a minstrel, voicing through his art the songs of the people.

He married twice; in the days of his youth, a French girl, and after her death, in the late years of his life, an American.

His last summer was spent in the United States. As his health failed, his thoughts turned more and more towards home, to Bergen with its seven mountains veiled in mist, and to his great house that he had built in the mountains. He wrote to a friend:

"Come with me to the land of the midnight sun. We will breathe in the spirit of the rocks and pines, and of the brave free air of Thor and Odin and the heroes of Valhalla. Norway, Norway, my heart is there—joyfully I follow."

Soon after he wrote, he went home to the land he loved. He ended his days, as he would have wished, on his own estate, the beautiful wooded island with the splendid views of Norway's mountains. Two great men of Norway spoke at his grave. One was Bjornsterne Bjornson, a great writer of Norway, and the other was Edvard Grieg, a great musician of Norway.

Bjornson's words were these:

"Ole Bull became the first and greatest festival in this people's life; he gave us self-respect, the greatest gift possible at the time. . . . He was a celebration himself, majestic, fascinating, as he walked among us, and a gesture of his hand, a look, raised in him who received it a holiday mood."

But it was Grieg who best summed up what Ole Bull had been able to do for his country. Grieg stepped forward and placed a laurel wreath on Ole's grave. Then he solemnly spoke:

"Because more than any other thou wast the glory of our land, because more than any other, thou hast carried our people with thee up towards the bright heights of art, because more than any other thou wast a pioneer of our young national music, more, much more than any other the faithful, warm-hearted conqueror of all hearts, because thou hast planted a seed which shall spring up in the future and for which coming generations shall bless thee—with the gratitude of thousands and thousands, for all this, in the name of our Norse memorial art, I lay this laurel wreath on thy coffin. Peace be with thy ashes!"

THE STORY OF HENRIK IBSEN

HENRIK JOHAN IBSEN

1828–1906

Henrik Ibsen was Norway's first great writer. His early life was poor and difficult. It was lived in a remote Norwegian town far from the world's centers of thought and learning. Yet Ibsen's imagination was rich, his thinking bold, and his hatred of evil so deep and intense that he overcame all the difficulties and wrote many plays that stirred up people's thoughts. Because of him, the people of Norway and of the world were able to go forward in their thinking.

CHAPTER I

BOY OF NORWAY

Skien in Norway is a small and isolated town. At the beginning of the last century, it was a town of about three thousand souls, a town of ships, cataracts, and lumber mills. These lumber mills filled the air constantly with sounds of screaming saws. There was no escape from these screaming saws except on Sundays when the mills were quiet. Then the cataracts took over; and to most of the towns-people, their dull roaring was the sound of Sunday, gloomy and stirring, like a sermon in the village church.

In the center of the town, on the village square, stood the church, the town hall, the prison, and the madhouse. Of these buildings the most interesting was the church. There was nothing unusual about it on the outside, but inside there was a softer light, a gentler and kindlier air, and the roar of the waterfalls was less. The thing that was fascinating about this church, at least to the children who came on each Sunday morning, was that up at the front, near the altar, and suspended from the ceiling, there was a large and heavy-limbed stone angel. This stone angel held in its hands a bowl for water used in the ceremony of baptism. On those Sundays when there were children to

74

be baptised, the angel was lowered slowly into the midst of the children and parents. It descended gravely with a ponderous dignity that suited a representative of Heaven.

One Sunday in winter, a certain family of Skien sat in their accustomed places in the white church. The father was Herr Knud Ibsen, the mother Fru Marichen Ibsen, and there were four children. Of these children, the oldest was Henrik Johan who was six. Henrik was small for his age. He had lively blue eyes, black hair thick like a mane, and an extraordinarily handsome and expressive face. He sat watching the scene before him with the most complete absorption. The descent of the stone angel had always fascinated him. He loved the ceiling shadows among which the angel lived, the reflected dancing sunlight on the folds of its robes, the glint of water in the baptismal bowl. On this particular morning, as he watched, his mind sped away to what he had seen the day before as he had walked alone in the mountains that surrounded his village. Near the cataracts he had found an ice angel and an ice church and a baptismal bowl so glittering that it might have been cut from a vast diamond. He saw these things clearly in his mind. They were so beautiful and of such unbelievable splendor that he shivered and twisted on his seat. Then, in his keen pleasure, he laughed softly out loud. As soon as he laughed, people around him turned to look. At once Henrik's bright visions disappeared, and he felt queer, stiff, and self-conscious, different from all the others.

His mother nudged him sharply. "Henrik," she whispered, "stop acting queerly."

The boy tried to turn his attention back to the scene before him, but all of its charm was gone. He felt that

75

because of his laughter the people of the church were no longer watching the ceremony, but were looking at him in disapproval, and saying to themselves, "One would think that in God's House a boy's behavior could be seemly."

The stone angel was pulled again to its place among the ceiling shadows, and after a final hymn the service ended. On the way home, Fru Ibsen and Herr Ibsen walked together silently; the other children ran and talked together, but Henrik still miserably self-conscious, walked by himself.

At home, Henrik stamped in ahead of the others. He pulled off his coat, cap, and boots, and went to his room. This room was the best place in the house for him. There were several books in it. One big one called Harrison's *History of London* was nearly one hundred years old. It had pictures of churches, and castles, and streets, and great ships, and right at the beginning a drawing of Death with an hourglass. He hated this last drawing and thought it was horrid. In the room, he also had pencils and a large paintbox.

After he had come in and looked around at his things, Henrik sat down on the floor and pulled out the paintbox. He began to draw. He drew slowly with extraordinary concentration and carefulness. Soon, on the paper before him, a man was going together. Line by line, shadow by shadow, as clear as it could be, there was one of the town's councilors. Big hat, bushy eyebrows, scowl, frock coat, double row of buttons—there could be no mistake. When Henrik finished, he took scissors and cut out the figure. Then he mounted it carefully on a block of wood so that it could stand alone. He then took a large box that he had hidden

76

away in a corner and took from it other figures that he had made. He set all these figures in a circle and imagined them talking together.

As he looked at the new town councilor standing so straight, scowling and looking so like himself, Henrik doubled up with glee. He began to speak words for him, and as he talked, these words seemed so true and fitted the town councilor so exactly that Henrik could no longer contain himself. He laughed aloud. Then he spoke in turn for the other people he had drawn, and the more he talked, the more true and humorous the conversations appeared to him. Yes, these were the townspeople. Even the buttons on their jackets were placed rightly. Henrik was talking and laughing freely now.

It was at this moment that his mother came in to call him to dinner. She looked at him doubtfully. "Are you talking to yourself again, Henrik? I can't believe that it is good for you. Come out with the others. You will grow queer if you are so much alone."

He went out and ate with the others, but he was still trembling, and so said little and kept his eyes on his plate. After the dinner was over, he wanted to go to his room again, but because he was afraid of what the family would say, he stayed on.

On the day before, Fru Ibsen had taken a piece of wood rubbed smooth and had made from it a doll for Henrik's sister, Hedvig. She had finished this doll with the exception of the face which she had left for Henrik to draw in. Now she called him to her. "You must put in the face," she said. "But for the face, the doll is ready."

All the children looked with interest at the new doll.

She wore a dress to her ankles and a bright kerchief over her head. Her blank face amused them, and they smiled and laughed as they looked at her.

"Here, Henrik, take the doll," said Fru Ibsen. "Draw the face. We must have her both pretty and good."

Henrik took the doll from his mother and went off to the end of the room to draw in the face. He sat down on the floor and for a few moments studied the smooth blank wood. All at once, from somewhere outside of himself, awful insight or inspiration came. As he stared, he saw a hideous and grimacing face appear, a troll-like mocking face. This awful face on the innocent little doll startled him. What if he should really draw such a face! He picked up the pencil and his fingers moved swiftly. He sketched eyes, nose, and a smiling mouth. The doll looked like a little angel. The contrast between the face he was drawing and the face that he might draw appeared to him so mocking and humorous that it was all he could do to keep from sketching in the lines. Seeing in his mind this contrast, he was queerly fascinated. He laughed and held up the pencil. He must watch this face change.

At the other end of the room, Hedvig saw Henrik's expression and heard his laugh. "Now he's laughing again," she said.

Fru Ibsen looked up. "Draw a good and proper face, Henrik," she said.

Henrik's pencil stopped. He held up the doll. "Yes, look," he said. "I'm doing it as well as ever I can."

He quickly finished the face. It was smooth, smiling, entirely good. It was a proper face for a doll who would have a proper doll's life.

Henrik handed the doll to Hedvig, and she, delighted by its prettiness, threw her arms around her brother. "Thanks, thanks," she said.

The others crowded around to admire, and Henrik, smiling at all the praise, stayed to play. But, unhappily, this game progressed like most of the family games. It went smoothly and merrily for a little while; then things went wrong. It was Henrik who was not playing properly.

Hedvig stamped her foot at him. "Go away," she said. "You spoil the game."

Henrik went away. He went to his room and locked himself in. He was always surprised that all the games ended in this way. He sat first at the edge of his bed and kicked at his box of mounted characters. Then he sat down on the floor. He heard his brother and sister go outside to play in the snow. Soon they came throwing snowballs at the wall of his room and shouting that he must come out too. He listened to the laughter and the balls flying against the wall. He ordered them to stop and when they did not, he went storming out and demanded that they stop. After that, he went back again to his room and sat on the floor.

It was quite a long while before imagination came to young Henrik Ibsen's rescue. Then he remembered the walk to the church, the wonderfully brilliant snow, the stone angel of the church, the solemn babies in their ceremonial robes, the pastor's voice announcing the new names, Knud, Ole, Edvard, Gabrielle. Henrik settled on the floor and was absorbed and happy for the rest of the day.

Of all the names given that day to the row of babies, none would be famous. But his own—Henrik Johan Ibsen —was destined to go 'round the world.

CHAPTER 2

ST. JOHN'S DAY FESTIVAL

One evening Herr Ibsen had an exciting announcement to make. He called the children in from the garden, where they were playing.

The announcement was about the wonderful Norwegian holiday which takes place each year on June 23. Sometimes it is called St. John's Day, and sometimes Midsummer Day. It is the longest day of the year. The sun stays in the sky all of the day and most of the night. Even after midnight, one can still read a book out of doors because of the clear soft light. This long light summer day is celebrated by the people of Norway because, in their land, the winters are particularly dark and cold. The people celebrate the day with singing and dancing and with the lighting of great summer bonfires. They light these bonfires at the moment the sun goes down.

In the sea-coast town of Skien, there were many ship builders who used barrels of tar in their building. The empty barrels burned wonderfully with a noisy and fragrant blaze.

"What I want to say," continued Herr Ibsen, "is that

the company in our neighborhood will have something for the fires in addition to the tar barrels. Our neighbors have contributed a sizable old barge. And you, Henrik, are to ride on top of it with the fiddler. The company will swing off with it to the tune of the fiddle. How do you like that?"

Both Hedvig and Henrik shouted in excitement. An old barge was always a prize because it burned long and made a great blaze. It was usually carried off by a festive train, and a fiddler was hired to sit on top and fiddle away and make the crowd merry.

Three weeks later, the wonderful Midsummer's Eve came. The crowd of boys and young men arrived to carry the barge. They were all shouting and laughing. "Here we are. Here is the fiddler. Come on, Henrik. You are to ride on the barge."

Henrik climbed up and they were off. The fiddler sat in front. This fiddler was an old man who was a wizard with the fiddle bow. Swoop went the bow, and the notes came out, fast, leaping, excited, and playful. The young men carrying the barge began to sing to the fiddle. The people walking behind also sang, and the children skipped and tried to sing too.

So they went to the place of the Midsummer Eve's fires. This place was on a hill which commanded a view up the coast and out over the sea and the off-coast islands. The barge was put down on the hilltop. Young men and boys piled wood and barrels on top of it.

Then all the people sat around the woodpiles, and there was dancing and singing. The songs were wonderful old sagas, solemn and stirring. Some were chants telling of the deeds of the heroes of Norway. And all the while the sun was going down to the rim of the sky. As it went down, it grew red and slowly turned the sky orange and red and gold. And now, at last, the moment long waited for was near. The light on the hilltop where the people sat was growing dim.

"Be ready to light the fires," the young men called out. "Watch the sun."

"Watch the sun," came the call from the next hill.

Like echoes came the calls from other companies. "Watch the sun. Watch the sun. Watch the sun."

The sun was a huge red ball now. One edge was over the horizon. Then suddenly it was gone.

At once the fires sprang up. Henrik saw them, first his own of fierce and fiery splendor. Then almost at the same moment, he saw the others, all up the coast and on the high cliffs and out on the islands. How beautiful they were soaring up to the sky! The distant ones were like big new stars. Henrik felt like jumping up in the air in high leaps and singing. If he had been older and able to write down what he felt, his words would have been something like these: "Oh wonderful night of the fires! St. John's Night. Midsummer Night. Night of the longest day of the year. Let the fires call back the sun, bringer of light and warmth!"

The fires blazed. How roaring and splendid in the twilight! Around some of them people danced and sang. Down below the hill, people had come up in boats to watch and to join in the singing.

Henrik, as was his custom when he was deeply stirred, went apart from the others to watch. The barge and all the tar barrels were burning now. They still held their shapes.

82

They looked like magic things, a barge and barrels made of fire.

This wonderful night was one of the last happy events in Henrik's boyhood. Not long after it, life changed completely for the Ibsen family.

Herr Knud Ibsen had always been reckless in business, liking to speculate in the lumber markets. He lost all that he had and could not even manage to keep the beautiful house with its gardens and rose hedges. The family moved to a poor farm at Venstob.

Henrik had to go to a school for poor boys. This school was in town, and every day there was a two-mile walk over the muddy road to get to it. He dreaded meeting friends from his former school.

"Where do you go now?" they asked. "You won't learn much there."

Sometimes as Henrik grew older, his father would talk to him. "Soon you must work," he said. "What do you want to do?"

"I would like to be an artist," Henrik answered.

Herr Ibsen scowled. "That is impossible," he said. "One cannot live by being an artist."

Another time when the same question was put to him, Henrik answered, "I want to be a doctor."

"That is also impossible," Herr Ibsen answered. "The training is too expensive. But perhaps in the future we can speak of it again."

The years passed and the Ibsen family continued to live the restricted poor life on the little farm. Herr Ibsen managed to support the family by selling ships' cargoes in the markets of Skien, but he could not again provide the big house, or bountiful food, or hospitality, ease, and light-hearted gaiety.

When Henrik was fifteen, his father talked to him again about working. "At one time you wanted to be a doctor," he said. "I have heard of work that is similar. It is in an apothecary's shop in the town of Grimstad." Herr Ibsen hastened on. "It is necessary that you take care of yourself. It is all that I can do to take care of the four other children. You are the oldest. The apothecary will provide food and a room in addition to the salary."

That night Henrik Ibsen walked alone through the dark streets of Skien. Though the hour was late, the sawmills were still running, filling the air with their screaming sounds. As Henrik walked and knew that he had no choice but to obey his father, it seemed to him that the sound of the saws was like his life, full of hard and harsh things, protest, storm, and revolution.

"What is Grimstad like?" he wondered. "I hate the name. It is ugly and grates on the tongue and in the ear."

He continued to walk, seeing his town, the church, the prison, and the madhouse, and hearing the sounds of the saws and waterfalls. Now that he had to leave, he longed to stay with what he knew. He kicked angrily at the small stones in his way, but after his anger was spent, he went home quietly, knowing there was nothing at all that he could do to change the plans that had been made for him.

CHAPTER 3

GRIMSTAD

Grimstad was smaller than Skien and more lonely. It faced into the east winds and looked out on a bay filled with jutting naked rocks. There were no street lights, or even lamps in the houses to make the windows bright. If at night a visitor went stumbling down one of the narrow streets, he would look in the shadeless windows and be glad for the homemade candle that burned upon the table.

Henrik came to this town in the month of January. The winds swooped in over the rocks and beat at the somber red houses. He held his jacket close around him. The wind drove the cold into him in long fierce gusts. Once he could not keep his feet and had to run before it helplessly as though he were a stick or a leaf. Down the frozen paths he went between the forlorn buildings and came finally to the shop where he was to work. As he hesitated a moment before the door, two old women whom he had passed turned to look at him.

"Who is that?" the one asked.

"It must be the apothecary boy," the second answered. "I heard he was coming. He is called Henrik Ibsen."

"He looks too small," the first woman said.

"Nevertheless I think it is he. He is fifteen, an age old enough to be working. He looks queer, his face so pale, and with that shock of black hair."

As the two talked, Henrik had gone into the shop where he was to work. He had known it would be poor, and yet its extreme poverty surprised him. The room was small and dark even in the middle of the day. The ceiling was so low that one could reach up and touch it with one's hands. There was one window of little panes of glass. He stood uncertainly, glad at least to be in out of the wind. In a moment, the apothecary came in from a dim room beyond.

"Welcome, Henrik Ibsen," he said. "You have come in good time. The day's mixing is yet to be done. Take your things upstairs. You will have a cot in the room of my two sons. Then come down. Here I have apron and pestle and bowl. I will show you how to make the mixtures."

"Yes, Herr Apothecary," Henrik answered. He went up a flight of dim and narrow stairs and put down his things, the few clothes and the box of books that he had brought from home. The attic room was bare and cold. But the thing that was wrong about it in his eyes was not this bareness and coldness, but the fact that he must share it with the two boys. If he could only have a place of his own, his own table, and a candle to light at night.

But he said nothing and did as he was told. In a moment he went down the narrow stairs into the dim shop.

The apothecary was cheerful. "Tie this around your middle," he said, holding out a black apron to Henrik. "Put these dry herbs in your bowl. Reduce them to powder. See to it that the powder is smooth and fine."

Henrik sat on a stool and mixed herbs in a bowl.

The apothecary then gave careful directions for several mixtures. After a few minutes he went out and left Henrik alone. Henrik sat on a stool behind the counter and worked the wooden pestle around and around in the bowl. His thick black hair fell over his face, concealing his dark and brilliant eyes. He looked so small, dark, and forlorn perched there in the dim room that he appeared actually to be what he once had been called during the years of childhood, "an elf of darkness." He worked through the afternoon. The wind outside did not grow less in fury, and as the boy listened to it, he was glad for its uncontrolled wildness.

"A hurricane is in my soul," he told himself.

His arms and shoulders began to ache with the unaccustomed exercise, but the dry herbs were still piled up high before him. Towards evening the dreams that had so many times helped him in his childhood came to his rescue. He saw himself as a little wizard pounding out and mixing magic powders. They were rainbow colored, of melting and enchanting shades. Merely by swallowing a dose, one could get a grip on the world. This dim shop was not his right place in the world. Henrik Ibsen knew that. Nor did he belong in his father's house in Skien. His mind raced and in imagination he saw the world spread out before him, all the glittering and wonderful cities where successful men lived. He saw himself, not small, or dark, or queer or poorly dressed, but tall and splendid with the important people of the world bowing to him. Then as the dream faded, and he saw himself once more as he really was, bent over the wooden bowl in the miserable room, he felt such despair and fury and hopelessness that he put down the bowl abruptly, and losing control, beat on the table with his hands.

"I must find my right place, I must, I must," he cried out.

The sound of his voice startled him. He was silent again, all the feelings and thoughts locked up tightly in his heart. He began to work, and worked until night came. When the family came in, he ate with them but was too tired to talk, and after the light supper he went up to bed. He had no energy left to desire his books or his own lighted candle.

In the months that followed he grew accustomed to Grimstad. He became used to the wind, and the gloom of the shop, and the long hours of work. His muscles strengthened, his arms and shoulders no longer ached from the pounding and mixing. His mind turned hungrily to his books, and in the hours that were his own, and these came usually only after midnight, he stayed below in the shop and read and studied by candlelight.

He did not mix with the people of the town. On Sundays they saw him going off by himself to prowl through the forests and the mountains. It was reported that he liked to sit alone in a stone cairn in one of the seaside cliffs, staring out to sea, or drawing pictures in a notebook that he kept.

"He is spectral," the people said, "like a ghost, always alone and liking those remote places apart from people."

The second year at Grimstad was harder for him than the first. He had always liked to keep clean and neat in a particularly careful precise way. Now his one suit of clothes became stained with the drug mixtures. There were many odd yellow and green spots. He hated these spots and the clinging drug odors. He had no overcoat for the cold winter, and for a long time no warm underwear, or even socks to wear. When the winds blew and the ice and snow piled up, he stayed in as much as he could. When he had to go out, he ran as fast as he could so that he might be warm again.

And then one day something wonderful happened to him, something that would help him on his way. In the customs office, down at the edge of Grimstad harbor, a new young man was working. His name was Christopher L. Due. He had been curious about Henrik Ibsen ever since he had heard certain reports about him, so now, on this lonely afternoon, he decided that he would go and seek him out.

"There's no harm in finding out about this Henrik Ibsen," he thought.

He made his way to the apothecary's shop, and pushing open the door, went into the gloomy small room. At first, in the dim light, he could see no one. He thought the place was empty and that the assistant must be in the next room. He knocked on the counter and at that, there was a movement behind a tall prescription case. A short young man came forward. His face wore an impatient expression as though he were being called from something that was important to him.

"What do you want?" he asked.

"A nickel's worth of plaster," Christopher Due answered.

Henrik found the plaster, and wrapping it quickly he handed it across the counter.

"I'm new here," Due said. "Can I come by in the evening and talk? I find things dull."

To Christopher's surprise, Henrik Ibsen did not hesitate. "Yes," he answered. "Yes, of course. We can talk here in the shop."

That night Due came to the shop at nine. Henrik was still working, compounding an evil-smelling dark powder. The shop was lighted by a few candles which did little to drive away the thick gloom of the night. Ibsen's eyes were brilliant. "I'll finish in a moment," he said.

Ten minutes later the two were talking freely. Ibsen saw at once that here at last was someone he could talk with and he responded with enthusiasm.

"What do you do here?" exclaimed Due. "You'll turn into a troll in all this gloom. Unless, that is, you get dried up first by one of your powders, or changed into something frightful. How long have you been here?"

"For one year," Henrik answered.

"There's no one around that I can find," Due answered. "No one, that is for you. I hear that you read."

"Yes, I brought books from home."

"Do you know," Christopher went on, "I also like to read. I even write a little, poems, and small articles. Before I came out here, I went to the newspaper in Oslo. I suggested that I be the paper's correspondent from here."

"And are you?" asked Ibsen.

"Yes, of course. They had nothing to lose, and sometimes things turn up in the most unlikely places. What place could be more unlikely than this?" Due stood up, and stretched his arms up over his head. "Ugh," he said. "Grimstad is as forlorn as Norwegian towns come."

"Shall we go out and walk?" Henrik suggested.

"No, thank you," Christopher answered. "I prefer your cave. It is much to be preferred to walking. We might fall into the sewers. I don't know them all yet."

The two sat down, and as they talked, Christopher Due found that his friend had free new bold views of life, and that his manner of talking was gay and spirited. "Of course you write down your thoughts," he said. "It could not be otherwise. You must show me what you do."

Henrik laughed. He wanted to bring out his notebooks and show them to this new friend, but he had kept them hidden and secret for so long that he could not bring himself to do it.

"I write some, yes," he said. "I will show you another time."

Christopher left at midnight. He walked home slowly, taking care to avoid the open street drains that he had talked about earlier. The night was dark, but the dim radiation of northern lights somewhat lightened the blackness and now made walking possible.

"To think," Due exulted, "that such a person is here in this town. I won't mind anything now."

He could not know that his new friend would some day be famous all over the world, and that his own name would be known because of this friendship.

CHAPTER 4

IBSEN WRITES A PLAY

The spring winds tore over Grimstad. They set the boats
in the harbor to rocking and plunging. They roared over
the little houses and made the townspeople who had to go
out hold tightly to caps and cloaks and scarfs. Christopher
Due and Henrik Ibsen were walking up the coast, and the
violence of the winds made it difficult for them to keep
their feet. Ibsen in spite of his slight appearance enjoyed
the turmoil.

"Look," he exclaimed, "how magnificent it is! See how
the water boils and seethes! See how the wild black hawks
swoop down the wind."

They came to a rock cairn that was a favorite place of
Ibsen. This place gave the two friends a perfect shelter.
Vast rocks surrounded them on three sides, and there was
a jutting shelf overhead.

"So you like a storm world," Due said after he was
comfortably seated. "I like it too when I am inside snug
and warm by the fire."

Ibsen laughed, but did not turn his eyes away from the
roaring ocean. "Storm is congenial to me," he said. "In
Skien where I was born, there was always the rushing roar

93

of waterfalls and the scream of sawmills. Their turbulence is in me."

He turned to his friend and spoke with great seriousness. "When I see how silent Norwegians are, how they lock up all difficulties in their souls, I feel as though I would like to start a revolution to get some of the hard things expressed. I am like my countrymen. My battles also take place in my soul. It would be better, I think, more healthful, to get them out in the open. For me, talk with you is good, a treat. My temper and anger slink away as we talk. I think it would be so for all of us. It is the locked-up stubborn Norwegian-ness that is bad."

"Of course, you are right," Due answered, "but there is nothing to be done. You cannot change Norwegians."

Each took a hard roll and a piece of sausage from his pocket and ate with enjoyment. Both Due and Ibsen were so poor it was difficult to buy even such small lunches.

Some months later, there happened one of those small events that at the time did not appear to be important. Christopher Due brought one of his poems to Henrik. The poem was called *Sunset*. Ibsen was interested at once.

"It is good," he said after he had read it. "We have so little poetry of Norway."

Then suddenly, he too wanted to show his friend something that he had written. Due had often asked of his writing, but Henrik had always felt too embarrassed and self-conscious about showing it. But now he took his notebook and handed it to Due.

"Here is one of mine," he said. "It is called *Autumn*."

Christopher Due read the poem, and as he read, he saw that Ibsen's poem was much better than his. "Yours is incomparably better," he said. "You must let me have it. Perhaps I can set it to music."

When he reread the poem at home in his room, he decided to send it to the newspaper in Oslo. "It can do no harm," he thought. "It is good enough to be printed." He looked at the signature of the poem, Brynjolf Bjarme. "Henrik is afraid of being laughed at," he thought. "At least it is a good pen name. It sounds Norwegian."

The next day the poem went off in an envelope to Oslo. Christopher Due did not tell Ibsen what he had done and during the following days his thoughts were always with the little poem. When the answer finally came, it was a copy of the Oslo newspaper. There printed in bold type was the poem *Autumn*, by Brynjolf Bjarme. Christopher Due raced with it to the apothecary's shop and spread out the paper before Ibsen. He said nothing while Ibsen looked over the paper. Ibsen did not see the poem at first. When he did, he turned quite pale with emotion.

"Look," said Due, "what did I tell you? Your poem is good. Here it is printed in the Oslo newspaper."

Ibsen took the paper and folded it carefully. All the afternoon, as he worked, he could not keep from looking at it. Indeed the paper had such a magic healing power that he did not see the darkness of the shop, nor its poorness or dinginess. The drugs that he mixed were fairy potions, rainbow colored and of the most extraordinary power. Brynjolf Bjarme was desperately poor. He was frequently hungry. He had no coat, and he wore clothes that were so stained by drugs that he suffered agonies of embarrassment when he removed his apron and had to go out and be seen by the people of the town. But this same

95

Brynjolf Bjarme had also written a poem, published in the important newspaper of the capital city. He had written other poems, many of them, in his notebooks.

So on this day, because of the poem, Ibsen's swift mind and imagination raced. The shop did not matter. He would escape and find his world. There would be clean clothes and whole shoes, a neat table of his own, candles, books, and pencils. And ideas would come in flocks ready to be written down. Serious thoughts would come, and there would be the poetry as well, the spirit of Norway's mountains, full of fantasy and beauty.

So Henrik dreamed there in the shop, and, because of the poem, he devoted more of his time to writing. He decided to try a new kind of composition. He began work on a historical play called *Catiline*.

Night after night he worked, writing by candlelight, stealing the hours from sleep. One night, just after it was finished, Christopher Due, and a new friend who had just come to town, came bursting into the apothecary's shop. Both young men were out of breath.

"We've been walking up the coast," said Due. "In this out-of-the-way corner of the world, nothing ever happens. We walk as though chased by devils because of boredom."

"Yes," said Ibsen's new friend, whose name was Ole Schulerud, "wake us up, Henrik Ibsen. What have you been thinking here in your cave? Is there a new poem?"

"No," Henrik answered, "but there is something else. Something just finished." He tried to conceal his excitement as he brought out the play. Then he lighted more candles and sat down with his friends.

"Shall I read?" he asked.

96

"Of course. What are you waiting for?" said Schulerud.

Ibsen began to read. "I must, I must, a voice is crying in my soul," he began, giving the first words of his hero, Catiline. He read well and with enthusiasm. The candlelight created a subdued yet comfortable atmosphere; the world of Grimstad faded out, and the scenes of the play rose up in its place. Henrik read for a long time, occasionally stopping to summarize so that he could get on faster. At last he finished.

Ole Schulerud was the first to jump up. "It's magnificent, Henrik," he said, clapping his friend's shoulder. "So you've written a play! Where did you learn of plays? And how did you come to try one? I like it immensely. It is something new for us. That first line, I like it. It is like your own struggles."

"We must make a clean copy," Christopher Due interrupted. "I have no doubt what must be done. One of us must take it to Oslo and show it to the publishers. We will sell it to the one who makes the highest bid."

"You must copy it, Due," said Ole Schulerud. "I will take it to Oslo. I am to go to the University soon and I can arrange my affairs to speed up my going."

During the following week, Christopher Due made the clean copy. He had a neat and handsome handwriting and was scrupulously careful to put in every comma and dash. The three friends together tied up the papers for Ole Schulerud to take to Oslo.

"I shall report to you within a few days as to the publisher," Schulerud declared. "We will want to consider his reliability as well as his success in reaching the public."

When, after some days had passed, the first letter came

from the city, the news was not exactly what Ibsen and Christopher Due expected. They tore the letter open:

"As you know, publishers are slow to take up a new form. For this reason, I believe that it will be better if we publish the book ourselves. I am ready to pay for the first printing and have already begun to make the arrangements. This new plan will make possible a rosy future for us. Henrik must come to Oslo, write two or three plays a year, and soon from their success we can travel, see the world, and have a suitable life of study and pleasure."

Henrik and Christopher Due read the letter, and, because they were both inexperienced in publishing and believed in the play, Schulerud's plan appeared sensible.

"Yes, Henrik," said Due, "you must go to the University with Schulerud. You will manage somehow. Why not go at once for the book's first appearance in the world?"

It was true that Henrik had made plans to go to the capital city some day to enter the University. But now the book's coming publication, the confidence and the encouraging words of his friend made him long to set out at once.

After the two friends parted, Henrik went to his room. For a long time he sat thinking. There was something in him, as Christopher Due had said, that was like the character of the hero of his play.

"I must, I must, a voice is crying in my soul," said Catiline.

Henrik Ibsen had always heard in his own soul the same insistent voice.

CHAPTER 5

OSLO

Grimstad to Oslo! Henrik Ibsen left by the little coast steamer. He observed with a poet's pleasure the myriad small islands and the blue bays leading inland. Though the spring green which would turn the coast of Norway into a fairyland of beauty was not yet come, still the blueness of sky and water and the bold lines of the coast hills and mountains had a striking splendor.

In Oslo, Henrik found the address that Ole Schulerud had given him, No. 17 Vinkelgata. It was a garret room, up long flights of stairs. Schulerud had the candles lighted, and a supper of bread, cheese and sausage spread out.

"Welcome, Henrik Ibsen," he said. "Eat, drink, and be merry. And after this feast, I shall show you a better one. Of course you know what it is—the book, our book, spread out in the bookseller's stalls. *Catiline* by Brynjolf Bjarme. It is a wonderful sight."

Henrik sat down before the small table. The garret room was as small as the one he had lived in in Grimstad. Yet, how different this one appeared to him! How friendly! How high above the city streets where so many people walked! The April winds were gentler too, not shrieking and wild as they were out on the mountains and on Grimstad's reefs.

"You are a genie, Ole," he said. "You've conjured it up. It's like a palace."

"Well, hardly," Ole Schulerud laughed. "But we will see real palaces soon. The play will be a success. You will write another, and another, and another! We'll all be rich and famous. We'll go to the Orient in one of the big boats. We'll see the show places of the world! But come, you can't take so long over bread and cheese. You must see the book and how it is spread out in the stalls in the company of the important writers from Denmark."

Henrik laughed, finished the cheese in a hurry, and the two of them went out into the streets of Oslo. The shop windows were brightly lighted. There were many people walking about and talking. To Henrik Ibsen's surprise, these people appeared to have nothing to do but enjoy themselves. He looked into a large pastry shop and saw crowds sitting around at the little tables, drinking chocolate, eating confections, and talking and laughing.

"This way, around the corner." Ole Schulerud was saying. "In one moment, you will see."

And there it was—suddenly! Ibsen stopped short and felt his heart grow tight and hard in his chest. The book-stall was large, and there were hundreds of books spread out. A glowing lamp swung over the stall and lighted up all the titles and the colored bindings. Ibsen's book was in the center, new, clean, and bright. There it was, having a new and separate existence of its own, not at all like the pile of sheets copied so lovingly in the dim room at Grimstad. Neither said a word. They watched the people come and go, pick up some of the books, and go again. No one asked for *Catiline*. But what matter? There it was, ready to be discovered. It was only a matter of time.

All of these first weeks together in Oslo were rich and full, with their own special excitement and charm. Schulerud's allowance paid the rent and for their dinners, which they took in a boardinghouse or in one of the many lighted cafés. Although Ibsen was busy studying for his University entrance examinations, he could not have enough of the crowded streets, the people, and the café life. He liked to take a table, sit watching for hours at a time. When he came at night to the garret room, Schulerud greeted him gaily.

"Herr Student Ibsen," he said. "Did you stuff yourself with learning today?"

"I am learning of Italy," Ibsen answered seriously. "Professor Heltberg is in love with it. He spreads out a feast of reason. He shows the arts of other countries as incomparably rich. It is only Norway that is so poor." His blue eyes gleamed. "We are a troll-ridden land. Our thoughts are of legends and fairy tales. We must give more attention to the souls of men, the struggles that go on in the silence. Last night I wrote a poem called *To the Poets of Norway*. The words are something like these. 'Less about the glaciers and the pine forests, less about the dusty legends of the past, and more about what is going on in the silent hearts of your brethren.' I feel as though I'm waking up and must say these things."

"You will do it," Schulerud said seriously.

Ibsen became a member of the students' literary society, read poetry, and began to attend lectures in literature and

101

philosophy. So wonderful was this world of literature to him that he gave most of his time to it. As a result, he failed in his examinations for the medical school.

During all of these months, Henrik and Ole Schulerud had managed to live on Schulerud's allowance. This allowance was enough for one, but when two tried to live on it, of course there were difficulties.

"All of this can't last much longer," Schulerud would say to his friend. "The people will soon discover the book. It will sell, and we will have money again."

When the dinner hour came, the two friends dressed carefully and went downstairs. They wanted the people of the house to think they were going out to buy dinner in one of the bright restaurants. They walked for an hour or so, long enough for the dinner. Then they would stop in one of the inexpensive shops, buy herring, bread, and perhaps coffee. Then they would go back to their rooms to eat from the paper bags.

"There is nothing wrong with herring and bread," Ole Schulerud would laugh. "Soon the play—"

"Don't say it again," said Ibsen.

The fact was that the first copies of *Catiline* still lay on the bookseller's table. The covers were no longer fresh and bright. When Ole Schulerud and Ibsen walked by the bookstands, each looked and said nothing. Then one day, when there was no money to buy even the herring and bread, Ibsen packed up most of the copies that they had, two hundred of them. He loaded them in a big box and went off to a huckster and sold them for wrapping paper. When he came in, he said nothing to Ole, but handed him the small sum of money. That night the two friends ate well.

Henrik bought a special and favorite cheese to give solace to the paper-bag feast.

About this time Ibsen sent in a play that he had written to the Oslo theater, and to his wonder and delight, it was accepted and plans made for three performances. When the performances were given, Henrik sat in the back of the theater. He hid both before and after the play and was so miserably conscious of its weaknesses that he was shaking and ill.

"I hid in the darkest corner," he told a friend later. "It was terrible."

Just at this time Ibsen heard of the plans of the great Ole Bull, for a Norwegian national theater. He was excited. How wonderful to have a Norwegian theater! A place to present the old thrilling romances, the history and poetry of Norway! A place also to present the serious things, the ideas, thoughts and criticisms of life! Henrik sat down and wrote an article for the newspaper. It was about Ole Bull's theater. His own strong feeling and desire went into the article. If such a one as the great violinist would get the theater started, Norwegians must be forever grateful. It was a great opportunity.

Later Ole Bull read the article. He asked about the writer. When he was told about him, and about the plays already written, and the one play performed, he asked to meet Ibsen. So the meeting came about. Norway's most famous man met a future great man of Norway.

"So you are Henrik Ibsen," said Ole Bull smiling. "I know of what you are trying to do. It is what I also think is important. Let me tell you of my ideas."

The smiling Ole sat down and talked to Henrik of his

103

dreams for the Norwegian theater. He was wonderfully winning as he always was, and was able to put the dark shy young man before him at ease. When Ibsen in turn talked of his ideas, Ole Bull listened gravely and intently. At last he stood up and put his hand on Henrik's shoulder.

"I want you," he said, "to be the poet of the first theater of Norway. It will have for its purpose the development of Norwegian talents, in writing, in music, and in acting. It must do great things for our beautiful country."

CHAPTER 6

WORK IN THE THEATER

Ole Bull made good his promise. The first theater of Norway was to arise in the old League city of Bergen, and Henrik Ibsen, inexperienced, untried, was to be resident playwright.

The two men made the trip together by steamer. Once, as they stood admiring the scene before them, Ole Bull looked up at the bright and swiftly-changing cloud banks. "How beautiful our land is!" he exclaimed. "Incomparably beautiful! But our people are too much isolated in their valleys and cloud lands. They live apart from the thought and progress of the world."

"I know," Ibsen answered.

The two men did not talk as the steamer entered Bergen harbor and tied up at the small wharf. Each was too busy enjoying the lively scene spread out before his eyes. To Ole Bull, it was a return to dearly-loved scenes; to Henrik Ibsen it was the place for the beginning of his work. The little picturesque city was dreams, and opportunity and challenge, at the same time, both wonderful and fearful.

A few hours later, introductions were made, a room was found near the theater for Henrik, and he met the directors of the theater, a board of men chosen because of their interest in the new venture. Ibsen's position was vague. He was to be theater poet and stage manager as well. He must write a play each year for the theater's anniversary program, and would help in choosing plays, staging them, and coaching the actors.

As long as Ole Bull stayed in the town, there were no difficulties. He brought with him always an air of celebration, and people worked with him, swept along by the atmosphere of dazzling promise. On the first theater evening, Ole Bull played his concert violin and the people were put under a spell both by his personality and his brilliant showy music and did not think to question the theater or its program, or the vast amount of work that would be necessary for its working out.

After a few weeks, Ole Bull left, and at once excitement went out of the air. Henrik Ibsen tried to take over. His difficulties began at once, for he was not tall, handsome, smiling, and genial, nor polished by success and contact with the important people of the world. Instead, he was green as grass, uneducated, without theater experience of any kind. Ibsen's first play for the new theater was to be given in January. He had worked for so many hours and in so many ways upon it that he no longer knew whether it was good or not. He had planned the scenes, drawing them out in pen and ink and water color on large sheets of paper. He had planned all the costumes, made many careful drawings, exact in every detail.

"I am back in the days of my childhood," he thought as he surveyed the careful drawings. "One difference is that I cannot order these actors around as I ordered the paper actors of my childhood. These will go their own ways."

Other nights he worked on careful stage directions. He did this by drawing a plan of the stage floor. He then made dotted lines to show where each actor must walk, and marked the places where each must stand to give his speech. He planned all the lighting effects and spent hours in the icy cold barn-like theater at night, swinging his lantern to see just what lights and shadows were needed to make the setting as he wanted. All of this work that he did by himself, though long and tedious, was easier than the actual rehearsals. It was hard for him to give directions to the green actors, to criticize the exaggerated and unreal manner of speaking and acting. Perhaps a few people appreciated his difficulties. A young lady who met him on the street one day said: "Well, Herr Student Ibsen, so you are going to teach Jacob Brun and the others how to act? God help you and good luck!"

When the night came for the first play to be given, Ibsen was strained and nervous. He dressed carefully these days. He often wore lace cuffs cut in frills, carried clean yellow gloves, and polished his boots till they gleamed. It was as though he had to push out of his mind the Grimstad days, the painful embarrassing days of the thin, drug-stained suit. After he was dressed, he delayed his going for as long as he could, and then, throwing on a black cloak, he went out. The night was beautiful, cold and white with bright stars, a proper night, he thought, for the theater's first festival. The occasion was a great one for the new theater. There were new decorations, new lanterns, clean newly-painted chairs. All of the seats had been sold, and the people came in a gay and festive mood.

Ibsen sat in the back of the hall. There was nothing more that he could do now. Sets, costumes, talking, acting—he had worked over them all, done everything that he knew how to do. As to the play, which was called *St. John's Night,* well, he would soon see how it went. The people around him were talking. He heard one say, "We shall see if Herr Student Ibsen of Oslo has anything to show."

The curtain went up. The play began. Ibsen listened to the words that he had written come out. He wanted so desperately to have the play succeed, that at first it did appear good to him. It was not long, however, before he saw that it was not good. Nothing was right, neither the words, nor the acting. Soon he heard hisses and hoots coming from the corners of the hall. His humiliation was so great that by the time the first scene was over, all that he hoped for was escape. He must leave before the curtain came down to avoid all the people. He sat miserably and pulled his cloak tightly about him as though to shut out the hostility. His face was so strained and white that he appeared ill. So the first play in Bergen was to be a failure on his list of failures! He listened to the people of the audience. How they jabbered and laughed! He doubted whether they could even hear the lines. As he peered forlornly around him, he saw the crude barn-like hall, the audience in shawls and great coats, the laughing inattentive faces. It seemed to him that he could never bear to see any of them or ever to be seen again.

"I must hurry out," he thought. In imagination he already heard the critical, harsh, and uncomprehending words coming at him like swooping hawks.

He slipped out just ahead of the crowds. Only a few

saw him as he hurried to his room in the adjoining building. His small black figure was like a specter.

A woman who saw him whispered to her companion. "Look, there is Student Ibsen," she whispered.

"See, how he creeps in his cloak," said the second.

"God only knows why Ole Bull brought him here."

One can imagine how the next days were for Student Ibsen. On the streets, he walked fast, looking always worried as though he were hurrying in, away from people. He worked harder than ever, burying himself in work, and so managed to push the defeat back in his mind.

The directors did not consider the failure so great. In fact, in the early spring, they sent Ibsen with two of the actors on a trip to Denmark and Germany to look at other theaters, to see the world a bit, to collect ideas for the new Norwegian theater. Back in Norway, he worked harder than ever, scurrying at night between the theater and his room, always designing, planning, and writing.

In the second year at Bergen, he produced his own play and had a second defeat.

In the third year, when the time came for a play by the theater poet, Ibsen had suffered such humiliation that he tried to protect himself. He had written a third play, but he dreaded taking it to the board of directors. On the night before he must take it in, he sat in his room looking at the thick pile of paper that represented so many hours of work. As he thought of taking the manuscript in, the expression of his face grew stiff and tight. His entire body became tense. It was as though he were already bracing himself against the attack, against the terrible hooting and hissing and devastating criticism.

"There is only one way I can do it," he said to himself.

On the next day, when he went in to give the package to the directors of the theater, he appeared more worried and strained than usual.

"Herr Director," he said, "I was not able to prepare a play for this season's anniversary program. However, a friend in Oslo who does not wish his name to be known has sent a play to me. I do not venture an opinion on it, but the directors may find it suitable."

Ibsen handed over his play. He was so stiff and constrained that afterwards the director recalled this stiffness which was exaggerated even for Ibsen.

The directors read the play and found it interesting. "Tell your friend," they said later to Ibsen, "that the play is good and highly acceptable. Will he now wish to have his name known?"

Ibsen shook his head. "No," he answered.

When rehearsals began, the actors worked with the lines, trying to bring them out clearly with proper emphasis and meaning. Ibsen had decided not to work with these actors lest he slip and reveal his authorship of the play. However, at one of the last of these rehearsals, he could hold himself in no longer. He rushed angrily out on the stage.

"No," he shouted, "you are not reading the lines correctly. They must go like this."

He then gave the entire passage, speaking with extraordinary feeling and precision. When he had finished, he realized what he had done. He hesitated for a moment, then quickly apologized for his interruption and went off.

The incident surprised the director. Then he saw what it meant. The authorship of the play had been puzzling him. But of course, now it was clear. Herr Ibsen was the author. How else did he know the long passage and how else could he give it with certainty? The director asked Ibsen later to admit that the play was his.

"Yes," Ibsen answered. "I wrote it, but I do not want my authorship known. My name must not appear on the play program."

"If you want it that way, all right," said the director.

The play was given, *Lady Inger of Ostrat*. Like the others, it also failed. It did not hold the interest of the people of Bergen. Only a few people liked it.

"Certainly the play is not good," said one of these, "but it has striking lines and a real poetic feeling. It is full of real problems, real struggles that take place in the mind. But should plays discuss such things?"

"I don't know," answered the second. "Perhaps if the questions in our minds are talked about in plays and books, such talk may be a way of studying the problems and getting them worked out."

For Henrik Ibsen who did not know of conversations such as this one, the play was simply one more failure. But what he did not know at this dark unhappy time of his life was that failures do not matter. That is, they do not matter if there is in them any promise at all of success. The tremendously important thing was that he was learning— learning to write, to think, to reach for ideas. He was learning besides, from the bottom up, all the details of the theater craft, building, designing, lighting, the art of natural dialog, and natural direct expression.

Above all he could observe closely his audience. He could study what got over well to the people and what did not. In the end probably only Shakespeare and perhaps the French playwright, Moliere, would have such complete working knowledge of the complicated art of theater craft as did Henrik Ibsen. Some day he would have important things to say to the world and would have learned the difficult art of saying them so that they would get into the minds of thinking people all over the world.

CHAPTER 7

ESCAPE TO ITALY

January 1856 came. Henrik Ibsen had worked for five years in Bergen. Then suddenly and surprisingly it happened. Incredibly wonderful and heart-warming, there it was, the first success.

When he went inside on this fifth anniversary night, he felt at once that both audience and actors were in an inspired mood. The actors were gay and spirited, and the audience sympathetic and ready to listen. As Ibsen felt this spirit of the players and of the people of Bergen, he was immediately warmed by the general air of friendliness and geniality.

"Perhaps the play can go well," he thought. He took off his coat and put it away, not caring on this night to sit with it folded closely around him. With the same recklessness he put away hat and gloves, and did not want them by him to make possible a secret escape.

The curtain went up. For a moment only he braced himself. Then he saw that the wonder had happened. The play would indeed go well. It was called *The Feast at Solhaug* and the subject celebrated Norwegian history. The patriotic subject and the use of lyrical and stirring ballads and poetry appealed to the mood of the people. As Ibsen watched and saw how it was with his play, warmth and gratitude flooded his heart.

When the play ended, for the first time in Ibsen's experience, he heard cheers and loud cries for the author to appear. He was discovered in his dark corner and pulled up on the stage. Though he looked stiff and dark as he always did, yet most of the people could see beneath the stiffness and see his emotion and his great joy that such success could come to him. He bowed his thanks and gave a stiff speech.

"Ladies and gentlemen," he said, "your appreciation shall strengthen me in my work toward the aim for which I am striving, and which I shall attain."

These words of Ibsen deserve attention. What was this goal of which he dreamed and toward which he so constantly worked? It was certainly not an evening of success or even many evenings during which audiences would say kind words of a play that he had written. His goal was far more difficult to achieve. What he dreamed of doing and was determined to do was to write plays that would stir up the minds of the people of his country. The plays must tell of real problems. They must have bite and fire and push the people into discussions and arguments.

The people followed Ibsen home with the members of the orchestra. The winter night beauty went to everyone's head. There was singing and snowballing and finally to make an end to the evening a serenade given by the orchestra beneath Ibsen's window.

The play's success and the favorable and kindly feeling that it created warmed the rest of the winter months for

Henrik. He sent it off to Oslo and it was performed there and published, his first book since *Catiline*. When the published copies were first sent to Ibsen, he opened them in his rooms. He picked up the small book and studied it, and his eyes, usually so somber, shone with the intensity of his feeling. He sent a copy of the book to a good friend and with the book he sent some verses which told how he felt.

"My little book is to me a flower
Dear indeed to my very heart."

Life had been difficult for Ibsen for so many years that it is not strange that the printed book was dear to his heart and like a flower.

A turning-point in Ibsen's life came to him at this time because of the play's success. Pastor Thoresen of the Cross Church in Bergen invited the playwright to his home to discuss some of the ideas expressed. Ibsen met the pastor's eighteen-year-old daughter, Susannah Thoresen. Susannah was an unusually spirited girl. She had dark eyes, curly dark hair, a lively and gay manner. When she was very little, she was always making up imaginative stories and had told her friends that some day she was to be the Queen of Iceland. The young girl won Ibsen's heart at once.

"I liked your play very much," she said looking directly at him. "I also liked the play of last year."

Susannah was fascinated by the world of books and plays. She and Ibsen talked and were immediately interested in each other.

As Ibsen walked through the Bergen snows, hurrying between his room and the big theater, he now had someone else to think about besides himself. When questions came up that were puzzling, he imagined himself talking them over with her in Pastor Thoresen's big house. For Ibsen, used to his small room and his own company, the house was friendly and spacious, and the coffee and sweet cakes more than ordinarily festive, and Susannah's interest like the coming of a Norwegian spring after the dark winter.

The success of the play had further results. He had an offer from the theater in Oslo of a position as "artistic director" there. The salary would be larger, and there would be all the advantages that the capital city could give. He talked of the new position to Susannah. When he talked with her, the locked-up look left his face. When he first came to see her, she had laughed at this serious look.

"You look like a lion," she said, "a black one, with your black beard and your hair like a mane, and such a scowling expression. If I did not know you, I would never guess that you are a poet of Norway."

When the directors of the theater met, they voted to release Ibsen from his contract with them. They agreed that he was entitled to the position in the larger theater. He made the change in the summer, traveling over the high mountains, delighting in the splendor of the forests, the flower-filled valleys, and the musical fairylike waterfalls.

In Oslo, he took over the new duties with enthusiasm. He walked briskly down the handsome old streets, enjoyed the people, the life in the cafés, and most of all the feeling that he was director of the theater and had a free hand to work out his ideas.

And now Ibsen married Susannah. They had a fine new apartment, arranged neatly, and Ibsen had a table desk, set in the window, with his writing materials precisely laid out. He made many plans and wrote poetry which was free and joyous.

But unhappily for Ibsen in the Norway of that day it was not easy for a writer to sell his work. Books and plays were by Danes, not Norwegians, and thinking was in the Danish pattern of thought. He had had some success and had written plays that deserved attention, and yet he was unable to get support or recognition of any kind. His salary was low, so low that he had difficulty living on it.

"Is it always to be the same old story, struggles, poverty, and worry?" he asked Susannah in weariness.

He managed for another year. He was thirty-five years old now, no longer a young man, and there were still dreadful days when he had so little money that it was difficult to buy food and paper for the writing, and even postage stamps for his business letters.

"I work as hard as I am able," he said to Susannah. "We must go to live in Denmark where there is a literary life established, and where it is possible to sell one's work."

"It is a tragedy to leave one's own country," Susannah answered soberly. "Apply once more to the government. Support is always given to push ahead such work as yours. Surely the help will be granted now."

Ibsen had already applied for a government pension that was given to artists who show promise. Now he wrote another letter to the government.

"Of course the answer will be favorable," Susannah declared.

"I hope so," Ibsen answered. But when the answer came, there were only the words "No action taken."

Ibsen was alone when he read it. He turned white when he saw the words. Then all at once he was furiously angry at the inability of the government officials to see what he was doing. He stamped out of the apartment, not caring to talk with Susannah. He scurried through the streets, looking darker and smaller than ever. He felt that the people around him wanted to hiss, spit at him, poke him in the back with a stick. As he walked his fury grew until it was like a torrent in him. He wanted to attack the society that he knew, so full of prejudices, so blank and uncomprehending.

So he stormed, and was sick and hurt at the same time. At home, he gave the letter to Susannah, but would not talk of it. In this way five hard years were lived through.

And now, once more, as in the last year at Bergen, suddenly, surprisingly, a way opened for him. First, the University offered him a small sum of money for travel. The famous poet, Bjornson, talked to influential friends who increased the fund. And all at once, there it was, money enough for escape, money enough for a time of freedom, for independent thinking, for work not done under pressure.

"Be off," Bjornson shouted at Ibsen. "Go to Italy where there is sunshine and mildness. Stop stewing here in your black cauldron."

The arrangements were made, and Henrik Ibsen escaped to a gentler land. "I will send for you, Susannah, if things go well," he promised.

CHAPTER 8

PEER GYNT

A dark tunnel takes the train under the Alps and into Italy. The train shoots into total blackness. It is as though the traveler must hesitate, must erase all pictures from his mind in order to be ready for Italy. Suddenly, there it is, after the blackness—a land of golden sunshine. To Henrik Ibsen, it was like a festival. His land was still dark and ice-bound. Here the flowers bloomed, the air was mild, the breezes gentle.

When he came to Rome, Italy's great and ancient capital, he could not get over his amazement at the world of enchantment. He went to a little inn, left his bags, and went out into the streets. There were palaces, and monuments, statues, and beautiful splashing fountains everywhere. Each street was like an art gallery. There were many small garden restaurants where people sat eating, drinking wine, and talking.

"I've truly found another world," Henrik Ibsen thought. "It is rich and poetic beyond my dreams."

He dined alone in one of the small vine-covered inns, felt open and genial, and visited with the waiters. When he looked at himself in a wall mirror, he was startled to see how somber he was in his black frock coat. "I shall dress differently tomorrow," he thought.

And indeed he did. On the next day, Ibsen, who in the North, was neat and dark like a crow, appeared in an artist's velvet jacket, a loose shirt, and a large hat lined with gleaming blue.

"I will put you on, 'Blue Grotto,'" he said laughing and addressing the big hat.

He roamed the streets in his velvet jacket, absorbed the sunshine. For the first time in his life he felt relaxed, and felt all the tense cords loosen. When he wrote to Bjornson, he wrote briefly, "Here at last, there is blessed peace." He read poetry and gave himself up to its enjoyment, and could not see the sense of the constant struggles of the Northland.

A few nights after his arrival he dined with a friend from Norway, Lorentz Diedrichson who was a painter. The restaurant had a garden filled with small tables, and it was there among the vines and flowers that the two men sat. The waiter came to take the order.

"What does the 'Big Hat' want?" he said addressing Ibsen.

"I have what I want," Ibsen answered smiling. "It is the beauty of Italy."

The waiter appeared to understand. He shrugged his shoulders. "But one must have food," he said.

"I have escaped from a prison house of ice," Ibsen answered. "I have lived like a bear in a cave. Escape is enough."

He removed his big hat with the gleaming blue lining. The waiter looked at it in admiration. "My friends call it the 'Blue Grotto,'" Ibsen said. "We have blue grottoes in my country, but they are not for the head."

The waiter laughed. "Will the owner of 'Blue Grotto' eat now?" he asked. "Wine, spaghetti, cheese, a salad like a garden?"

Lorentz Diedrichson interrupted and gave the order. When the waiter had gone, he looked at Ibsen, sitting relaxed and genial in his chair. "You would talk forever, and I am hungry," he said. "Do you know for the first time, I see you looking like a poet. You have become like the rest of us artists, long-haired and lazy, a lover of talk and languor."

"I will no longer slash about," Ibsen answered. "I want to sit in the sun and soak it up and then go off to an art gallery to look at the statues."

At this point in the conversation, the waiter brought the food. Lorentz Diedrichson and "Blue Grotto" ate with relish. They both drank the Italian wine and broke the long bread sticks, and ate them with the cheese and salad. After the supper, Ibsen made no move.

"The Italians stay on and are in no hurry," he said. "Let us do as they do."

So the two Norwegians sat through the evening, listened to the Italians sing, and gave themselves up to leisure and the spell of the summer night.

"Heigh ho," said Ibsen at last. "I am going to my room. I shall walk for a while first, and look at the moonlight on the monuments, and make an end of today's sojourn in fairyland."

The two friends said good night outside of the inn, and each went his own way.

The weeks passed. Ibsen sent for Susannah and their small son, Sigurd. In the fall, they took pleasant rooms in Rome, and Ibsen felt ready to take up his work again. The first work to be written in Italy was a play called *Brand*. The writing went well. Ibsen wrote of it to Bjornson:

"I am working both forenoon and afternoon, a thing which I have never before been able to do. The place here is blessedly peaceful, no acquaintances, and I read nothing but the Bible. That is powerful and strong."

Later he wrote: "I am filled with such active strength and power, I could kill bears."

After *Brand*, which is considered a masterpiece, Ibsen wrote another play which was in a greater degree inspired by Italy. He moved out of Rome with Susannah and Sigurd and took a nest of rooms in the mountains, two thousand feet above the sea. He fitted up a study with a writing table at the window.

"Ha! I plan to write a gay comedy," he said one day. "So far from my readers, I am reckless."

He wrote through the morning and again through the afternoon. When he came out of his room, tired from the writing, he often called Sigurd. "Come, let us walk in the mountains and dream we are in Norway," he would say.

The play was *Peer Gynt* and it would be another masterpiece. It is a long poem, a fantasy, reckless, inspired, and playful. The hero is an old character of Norwegian fairy legend, a braggart and teller of tall tales. Ibsen had heard of this character when he had taken walking tours in the Norwegian mountains and had talked with the country people.

Now he used this character and made a story around him.

When *Peer Gynt* was sent off to Norway, it took root at once among the Norwegian people. From Norway, Bjornsterne Bjornson sent off a joyful letter to Ibsen.

> "Dearest Ibsen! I am so thankful to you for *Peer Gynt* that I do not remember any book during the years I have been an author which has so invoked my desire to give a warm handclasp for what I have warmly received."

One can imagine Ibsen receiving the warm letter from Bjornson. Success had come to him at last. It had been long in coming. He was thirty-nine years old, and it was time that his genius be recognized and the years of work have some reward. Now at last the Norwegian government voted him a poet's pension, and there would soon be an income from the books. The crippling embarrassing worry about the necessary things of life was about to end.

Ibsen walked in the Italian sunshine with Susannah and Sigurd and laughed and talked of *Peer Gynt*.

"That fellow *Peer Gynt* is an ugly brat," he said.

"Yes," Susannah answered, "but lovable and very fascinating. He will steal the people's hearts."

CHAPTER 9

NORWAY'S MOST FAMOUS MAN

Year after year, Ibsen refused to go back to Norway. Many wondered at this, for they knew that many Norwegians would welcome him. The early years, however, had been too bitter. The humiliations he had suffered in his country, the fears, and the lack of any understanding on the part of his countrymen, had put a wall of ice around his heart. He lived in Italy and in Germany.

Friends who came to see him were startled to see how he was changing. He had adopted a stiffly formal costume and now wore a double-breasted frock coat, long and black. He wore shining patent leather shoes, immaculate yellow gloves, a white satin tie, and a tall top hat. Because of his nearsightedness, he had to wear gold-rimmed spectacles. He appeared always correct, so carefully and elegantly dressed that some who saw him could not keep from thinking of the Grimstad days and the humiliations of the drug-stained suit. He must be trying, they thought, to bury those days in his present neatness and elegance. He had always been very short, and now, dressed so elegantly, and with his hair and beard making a ruff around his face, he looked lion-like, groomed, and bristling.

So at last Ibsen came home to Norway.

In other matters than clothes, he grew more precise and neat. He changed his handwriting, which had been untidy and straggling, into a small, firm, vertical hand. He wrote each tiny letter carefully with such extreme care that each word was like a little Chinese drawing. He drew penciled lines on unlined paper when he wrote, and then was careful to remove all the tracing.

He wanted to observe people, yet feared to talk with them, and so formed a habit of going to a café to study them. There he would sit, half hidden behind a newspaper, peering out at the people from behind the gold-rimmed spectacles. Nothing escaped his sharp observation—colors, buttons, shoes, gestures, facial expressions, and ways of talk.

His fame and wealth and importance for the world of thought grew. He was given many honors, and he liked to wear these symbols, all the golden crosses and the colored ribbons. On special occasions he looked ablaze with them all spread out on his coat. Perhaps his childlike love of these decorations was, like his fondness for elegant clothes, a way of telling himself that his bitter struggling days were gone forever, that he was no longer a nobody from a tiny isolated village.

The years passed, and as Henrik Ibsen grew old he longed for Norway. It was lonely always living in a foreign land. He dreamed of the shining glaciers, the mountains, and the blue sea. He had once written:

"What is life? A fighting
In heart and brain with trolls."

Perhaps it was time to return. He had fought the trolls

of darkness all his life. Perhaps the time of fighting was nearly over and he could take the beautiful and peaceful things. He was sixty-three years old. A line from his play *Brand* must often have been in his heart. "His native place is to a man's foot what the root is to the tree." It would be good to find roots again.

"We must go home," he said to Susannah. "We must visit Norway."

And so at last Ibsen went home. And this time, perhaps because he was old, and no longer so angry and bristling, he was able to find his place. His country, too, was growing up. Some of the isolation was breaking. There was a literature of Norway, and the people of the world knew this literature and, through it, something of Norwegians.

As the years passed, he became part of the life of Oslo. Each afternoon precisely at one, he took his promenade on the dignified old avenue Karl Johans Gade. The children always watched for him.

"It's time for Doctor Ibsen," they said. "Where can he be?"

"No, it's not one yet. In five minutes more, he will come."

In precisely five minutes, a short old gentleman appeared. The children smiled. "That's Dr. Ibsen," they said. "It's one o'clock. Dr. Ibsen is our clock."

The old gentleman would smile at the children from behind his gold-rimmed spectacles. His blue eyes lighted up and sent out bright gleams of blue. Then, as they skipped off, he stiffened up and marched off down the dignified street. He wore his black frock coat covered with decorations, his tall hat, white satin tie, and he carried in his small yellow-gloved hands, a gold-headed walnut stick. He was on his way to the Grand Hotel to take lunch alone, to drink coffee, and read his paper and observe people. He had one particular table and one particular chair which were his alone. No one dared to disturb him.

When he went into the hotel, he sat down, ordered his coffee, and read his newspaper exactly as he did every day in the week. How he enjoyed watching all the people, their expressions, and gestures! All the odd details of costume were as interesting to him as ever. For a while he sat behind the paper, upright and stiff, watching the scene. Then, as he became more and more aware of the eyes of people, he settled deeper behind the newspaper. This time he placed his silk hat at a careful angle. There was a little mirror in the top of the hat which reflected the crowd for him. He peered into this little mirror and studied the people he saw in it intently. How fascinating people always were!

Many honors came to the old gentleman. At one celebration, when he stood up to reply to the tribute paid to him, his mind went back over the past, all the times of difficulty. His words were these:

"I, the old dramatist, see my life remolded into a poem, a fairy poem. It has been transformed into a summer night's dream."

But even now at parties in his honor, Ibsen could not unbend for long. He could come into the room full of guests only for a few minutes at a time. Then the habit of shyness would catch up with him, and he would quickly shake hands and disappear, and only later, after a time of retreat in his room, could he find courage to reappear briefly again.

In 1899 came the greatest honor of his life.

The first Norwegian National Theater was opened. In the stately building, a great and distinguished audience came to see a play by Ibsen, and to acclaim the man who had given his life to work for a theater in Norway. But even on this great occasion, Ibsen went to the theater feeling both doubt and fear. He had always been unsure of the love of his countrymen. The years of failure had left their mark. Even his successes had stirred up public anger and contempt. So now he sat in a raised and gilded chair, garlanded with red and white roses. Yet he was afraid, and stared straight ahead, tapping nervously with his foot.

When the curtain went up, the principal actor came out on the stage. He motioned for silence, and then read a poem in honor of Ibsen. When the actor had finished, he ran over to the box, and with arms extended, shouted, "Long live Henrik Ibsen!" At once the vast audience was on its feet. "Long live our great poet!" the people shouted. "Long live Henrik Ibsen!" Over and over again they repeated the cry.

Henrik Ibsen stood up in his box and looked through tears at the sea of shouting people. Their affection and warmth and respect were unmistakable. So he had a warm place in their hearts! It was not only in their minds that they gave him honor. He did not know how to respond. The tumult continued. At last he seated himself, after falteringly raising his hand to the crowd, as though begging them to spare him. Only the lifting of the curtain for the second time and the actual beginning of the play, sufficed to bring the applause to an end.

Ibsen's play was then given. At the end of every act, the

people called him to the front of his box to receive their applause. But at the very end, after the final curtain, when they turned to give him their final honor, Ibsen had disappeared. A moment later he was discovered and brought back. On his reappearance, the audience rose in a roar of welcome. And this time the cheering was long and unrestrained, and the walls of Norway's first national theater resounded with acclaim for the man who had done the most to make the theater possible.

When the aged poet was at last allowed to leave, he walked slowly, visibly exhausted by emotion, bowing and smiling, down a lane of people which extended far out into the street.

The astonishing night ended. Norway had given her tribute to her greatest citizen.

THE STORY OF EDVARD GRIEG

EDVARD HAGERUP GRIEG

1843–1907

In Edvard Grieg, Norway had her first great composer of music. Grieg loved his land, the wild lofty mountains, and the deep flowering fjord valleys. He was able to express his strong feelings in music. Now this music is widely known and its springtime air and delicacy interpret to the world the fairy-tale beauty of Norway.

CHAPTER I

A STRANGE CHORD

One night in the seacoast town of Bergen in Norway, there was a crashing storm. The thunder rolled in the mountains, and the lightning streaked up across the sky in quivering flashes.

In the house at Number Two Strandgaten, a very small boy stood watching with his nose pressed against the window glass. He was five years old, but was so small that he looked even younger. He had blue eyes, and pale blond hair, and he wore a blue blouse that was slightly too large for him. His name was Edvard Grieg.

Usually little Edvard Grieg, like most of the children of Bergen, enjoyed the exciting storms, but tonight, because there was soon to be an evening party in his mother's house, he wished that the rain would go away. As he watched, the lightning flashed up the sky, and in that one moment, before the dark came again, he saw the huge forms of the mountains and all the houses standing in the rain.

The room in which Edvard stood was large, comfortable, and cheerfully lighted for the party. The most prominent piece of furniture was a black piano which stood against one wall. Piles of music lay on it, and a lamp near by threw an inviting light over the gleaming keys and dark wood. Edvard had been standing for some time with his back to the cheerful room, but now, there came a particularly long rumble of thunder which rolled in the mountains as though it were a vast ball knocked about by giants. He shivered, and turning from the window, he ran quickly to the piano. Standing on tiptoe, and using both hands, he reached up and struck a chord—five notes. The sounds jangled as if they did not quite fit together. He struck them again, and again listened intently. Then he smiled in fascinated delight, and, turning quickly, ran from the piano across the large room to the kitchen where his mother was helping to prepare food for the party.

The kitchen was full of good smells and interesting plates of food. Edvard's mother was having guests for an evening of music. Hot water steamed in big coffee pots. Sweet sugared breads sprinkled with almonds were spread out on a big platter, and a round cheese stood on its plate under an embroidered cover. A maid servant was setting out a pile of coffee cups.

As Edvard came in, Fru Grieg turned toward him and smiled. "I listened to your chord, Edvard, and the way you played it. It sounds a little like the storm, I think. Do you know when I was a child about your age, and before I could play or had any lessons in music, I liked to pick out tunes, one note at a time. But you do not try tunes, only those odd chords, darling. They are very interesting, I think. I must start your piano lessons soon. Will you like that? I think you have a talent for music."

Fru Grieg straightened Edvard's blue blouse and shook

her finger at him. "But in that case, you will have to work. You are too much a little dreamer of Norway."

As Fru Grieg turned again to the coffeepots, the rain blew in a noisy gust against the house. Edvard pulled a chair over to the window, climbed on it, and once more pressed his face against the glass. The rain was now pelting the rooftops, filling the gutters, and turning the waterspouts into waterfalls.

"Mother, will the people come?" he asked anxiously.

"And why not?" interrupted the servant. "If one were to stay in for the rain in Bergen, one would never see much of the town."

"Yes, darling, I know they will come," said Fru Grieg, smiling at Edvard's serious expression. "Do you know we are the rainiest city in Europe? But I like the sound, and the curtain over the world. It will shut us in tonight with the great Mozart."

But Edvard would be restless until all the guests had arrived. He loved these evenings of music and could not have enough of them. Usually he found a corner of the room and sat on the floor where he could watch the musicians. Music was always a wonderland to him, and he would listen with a sober dreamy intentness, following the melodies and smiling in delight when the notes pleased him. He particularly liked chords and harmonies, and liked to hear a simple songlike melody deepen and change as the various instruments took it up.

At this moment, there was a pounding at the door, and the first two guests came in shaking off the rain. They were two gentlemen. Each one carried a large umbrella and a fiddle case.

"Good evening, Fru Grieg," said one. "The trolls take so much rain!"

"Where can it all come from?" said the second, laughing.

Both gentlemen hung their overcoats on a coat tree in the hall, and Fru Grieg placed the dripping umbrellas in a stand.

"Did you see any of the others?" she asked.

"Yes, they're coming along, a square behind."

In a few minutes the others had come, and the large parlor was full of men and women talking.

"I have been reading of our Norse violinist, Ole Bull," said one, as he put out some sheets of music.

"He is astonishing," said another. "Whenever he plays his violin, he creates the wildest enthusiasm. He is like a sorcerer."

Fru Grieg interrupted the two gentlemen. "What do you think of his ideas?" she asked. "He talks always of Norse music for Norway. He writes in that confident enthusiastic manner of his. He says we must put Norway into music, the folk songs of the people, the sounds of the winds, and the roar of our waterfalls."

"But there is no music such as that," said the first man. "Ole Bull composes some, but I think his music is not good enough. It will not stand alone, apart from his playing."

"Sometimes," said Fru Grieg, "he talks of starting a Norwegian theater here in Bergen. Only the music of Norway would be played there, and only plays written by our countrymen would be performed there. I think, though, it is one of Ole's dreams. Where could he find such music as that and such plays?"

"All the same," said the first man, "he is a great man. He

has played in so many countries, Italy, France, England, and the United States. I think many people know of Norway only because of him. Perhaps someday, there will be a music of Norway, and a great literature of Norway."

"Yes, perhaps," nodded Fru Grieg. "And now, shall we get to our music of the evening?"

She opened the book of music which was in front of her on the piano. It was Mozart, a complete edition of the beautiful sonatas. Soon the Grieg house was filled with sound. The musicians played one sonata after another, and the graceful, musical melodies sang out.

During all of this time, Edvard was sitting on the floor in his corner listening. When Fru Grieg looked at him from time to time, she smiled to see how completely he lost himself in the melodies.

"He will surely be a musician," she thought. "If not, how could so small a boy sit without moving through the long sonata?"

Outside the house, the rain came down faster until it was like a torrent. It rocked the boats in Bergen harbor and drenched the gardens. It blotted out the islands, and the mountains that towered over the little city, and the long fjords that led inland. The thunder still rolled in the mountains, and once, during one of the crashes, Edvard went to the window to look out. Though he could not have put what he felt into words because he was only five years old and had not yet started to school, yet he knew, in his own way, that the music of Mozart which filled the room was not at all like what he saw. It was in no way related to the spirit of this storm land. As he looked, he heard clearly in his mind his chord that he had played earlier in the evening. It was this chord with its jangly notes and its strangeness that was like the scene before him.

The music was ending. The musicians put their violins back in the cases and folded up the music sheets. Edvard skipped among the guests while the maid servant brought in coffee and the interesting platters of sweet breads. For those who did not care for the sugared breads, there was the cheese under its embroidered cloth, and firm black bread to go with it.

After the guests had gone, Fru Grieg turned to Edvard. "It is late for you, darling," she said. "You must get to bed. How beautiful the Mozart music was! I could see how you liked it. I think we will begin piano lessons for you at once."

They went upstairs, and soon little Edvard was asleep.

On the other side of the rainy Atlantic, on this same evening, in a certain hotel room in New York City, a famous violinist rested after a concert that he had just given. It was the tall and smiling Norseman, Ole Bull. He was standing, looking at his famous violin which he was holding.

"I always play the folk songs of Norway," he thought. "I wish I had the musical knowledge to orchestrate them."

He laid down his handsome instrument. "Perhaps, some-day, there will come a musician out of Norway who can do what I cannot. He will grow up, loving our mountain won-derland, the splendid, noble views and fjords, like no other land in the world. But he will not be like me, a musi-cian without sound knowledge. He will have studied. He will understand harmonies. He will be able to put the spirit of the land into great and important music. I think such a man can give great happiness to the world."

137

CHAPTER 2

COMPOSING IS DIFFERENT

The piano lessons had begun.

In the parlor, during the bright mornings, the sunlight fell across the big piano and across the small figure of Edvard Grieg as he tried to practice. This practice was tiresome, all scales and exercises and counting. He could manage it for a short time. Then, suddenly, without any planning, he wanted to try a chord of his own, or a little song. He wanted to forget the bothersome lessons and to try a little of everything, just a note that he liked to hear struck over and over, or two notes played together with one finger. Or he wanted not to play anything at all, but to sit and stare dreamily into the sunlight and imagine a burst of the most glorious music coming out of the piano, and himself making it like a little wizard.

Usually, just when the picture was the most clear and wonderful, his mother would come in from the kitchen. "You are not getting on with your task, Edvard," she would say. "It is all right to dream, but only after the work is done."

Then he would start the scales again, and she would return to the kitchen. Fru Grieg, in secret, was charmed with the way Edvard explored the possibilities of the piano. She

Edvard loved the mountain country near Bergen.

was well trained in music, and she was certain that this constant trying of notes and combinations of notes indicated a musical nature. Now as she listened, she heard him make a mistake.

"Fie, Edvard," she called out. "F sharp, F sharp, not F."

At once he came running to the kitchen. "How did you know, mother?" he asked in the most complete surprise. "How can you tell?"

Fru Grieg laughed. "By my good ears," she answered. "Run back, try it for yourself. First the F, then the F sharp. I think your ear will tell you too."

Edvard did as she directed and heard at once that only

the F sharp would do. As he played on through the exercise, he could not get over her wonderful cleverness. It was very interesting how only the one note could be right. As he thought this, Edvard twisted on his chair, and smiled to himself, and had to try a chord again. First, two notes together, then four, and then with both hands five notes at once, the chord which is called by those who know musical terms, the "ninth." Edvard took a deep breath. How glorious was this chord of the "ninth"! One could listen to one note at a time, or to all the five sounds together. This chord was so interesting to little Edvard Grieg and so real that he could close his eyes and let himself go, and almost imagine that it was a place like wonderland, and that he could run around between all the delightful sounds.

Edvard was dreaming again, trying the intoxicating combinations of notes. Then the clock struck. The time at the piano was over. Quickly Edvard came out of his wonderland, and in a moment, slid off his chair, and was off, skipping outside where the sun and a bright mild day had long been calling all the Bergen children.

For there were two most wonderful things in the life of young Edvard Grieg. One was music, and the other was the great outdoor world of Bergen harbor. The mountains, the blue harbor with its wooded islets and many ships, the famous fish market, the piles of gaping fish, and the bearded fishermen who told stories of the sea. All these fascinated him. The fish and salt smells made him laugh and breathe deeply and screw up his nose.

On some afternoons, Edvard's father, Herr Alexander Grieg, drove his family out to the country. There were four other children besides Edvard—Maren, Ingeborg, John,

140

and the baby, Elisabeth. The country drives near Bergen were wonderful. There were the fjords, and the mountains, and the waterfalls. Everything was full of color in the sunshine.

School did not give Edvard as much as nature because he never was happy there or able to fit in well. When he first started to school, he hated it and could not get used to the confinement, the dullness, and all the tedious rules.

One day, when Edvard was about ten years old, he set out at the usual hour for school. It was a typical Bergen day of rain, and he had to go under his big umbrella. He went slowly, jumping the small pools and wading through the larger ones. When he came to a certain place where there was a gushing water spout pouring out its miniature waterfall, he stopped and examined it with interest. Suddenly there came to him the way to solve the problem of school. Two days before, a boy in his class had been sent home because he was too wet. Now, quickly, Edvard looked up and down the street, and seeing no one whom he knew, stepped directly under the waterspout. When he was thoroughly wet, he continued on his way. When he came to the school, the class had already begun, and the master looked up in annoyance.

"Edvard Grieg," he said, "what has kept you?"

Then he stared in surprise at the boy. For though Edvard had taken off his cap, coat, and galoshes, he looked as though he had just been pulled from a trout stream. Such streams of water poured from his clothes that in a moment the floor was covered with pools.

"What can have happened to you?" the master said, speaking with irritation. "You will have to go home."

Edvard nodded and left at once. He repeated this prank on several other days. It served his purpose well, and he felt very proud of this strategy. One day, however, he came wet through when there was scarcely any rain. The master became suspicious. A watch was set, and Edvard was discovered. He was punished, of course, but the whipping was not as bad for him as the dreary knowledge that there was now no way of escaping the prison-like school.

It was not long after the affair of the waterspout that Edvard did have a real success in the school. This was so unusual for him and was such a splendid triumph that even after many years had passed and he had become a man, he still liked to tell about it. Once at home, as a punishment for some offense, Herr Grieg had required Edvard to memorize the history of Louis XIV of France. He had recited the story to his father with all the details so that all the facts were fixed, firm and solid, in his memory. The very next day in the history class, the teacher looked at Edvard.

"Edvard Grieg," he said, "tell me something about Louis XIV."

Edvard stood up. He opened his mouth and the words poured out. He forgot nothing. The teacher was greatly astonished and could scarcely believe his ears. He began to turn the pages once more. "Tell me," he said, "who were the generals on the Black Sea under Catherine II?"

The other boys looked at Edvard, but for once, luck was with him. He swallowed and answered quickly in a loud voice, "Generals Greigh and Elphinstone." Edvard had known these names for a long time because his father had once told him that this officer, Greigh, who was a Scotsman, was quite probably one of his own ancestors.

The teacher clapped the book shut. "Right," he said. "For that you will get one and a star."

Such was Edvard's success, and it was so complete and dazzling that he felt like a general after a successful battle. The boys looked at him with a new respect. "How did you know about the generals?" they asked.

"I just knew them," said Edvard easily.

On another occasion a bad thing happened, and it was especially unfortunate because it came from music which was now what Edvard liked best of all things in the world. For many days at the end of the practice hours, he had been making up a musical composition of his own. It was based upon a German melody that interpreted an old legend of the Rhine River. Edvard had liked to take the melody and write variations on it. It was curious how his chords and harmonies made the German song turn Norwegian.

Edvard finished writing it one night in one of his music books. The last thing that he wrote was the title which he printed in large letters. *Variations on a German Melody for the Piano by Edvard Grieg. Opus 1*. Edvard liked the words, Opus I—the first work. After he had looked at it all completed, he had to play it again, and still again.

Fru Grieg came into the room. She smiled as she saw how far away Edvard was in his musical wonderland. "Darling," she said, "you are still too much a little dreamer. Go to bed now. There will be time for music tomorrow."

Edvard took the music book to school with him the next day. During the first class, he had trouble keeping his mind on the lesson. The notes that he had written and the carefully printed title were simply irresistible. He could not keep from taking out the notebook and showing it to a schoolmate. This boy did not at first believe that it was Edvard's work. He expressed surprise and interest in such a lively way that he attracted the attention of the master.

"What is the matter?" the schoolmaster asked.

"Grieg has composed something," the boy answered.

"So," said the master shrugging his shoulders. "Well, let us see it." He took the book and examined it and then called the teacher in the next room.

Grieg felt certain of a grand success. He thought that the teachers would see that this work of his was full of genius. At this moment, the second teacher left, and the first turning to look at Grieg, saw that the boys were crowding around him, asking of the composition. As the disorder grew, he lost his temper. He came down among the boys and seized Grieg harshly by the hair.

"Another time," he said gruffly, "bring the German dictionary and leave this stupid stuff at home."

So Edvard Grieg did not have his grand success. What he had begun with so much pleasure ended miserably. He sat at his desk, swinging his feet, and could not understand how it was that in the schoolroom nothing was ever right. He did not feel happy again until after school when he went walking down by Bergen harbor. Once there, the unpleasant thoughts flew away. There were the boats rocking on the water, the forest of masts, the fishermen, and the brown kegs of fish. Overhead, the sky was blue and vast, and the clouds sailed by slowly and lazily. Edvard sat down and watched them vanish over the mountaintops. And, after a while, when he went home, he went skipping and wanted to go to the piano to try music that would tell of the mood of the harbor, the clouds, the mountains and green islands.

CHAPTER 3

OLE BULL CALLS ON THE GRIEGS

Edvard was twelve years old, then thirteen, and fourteen, and by his fourteenth year, he was playing and composing with marked distinction. During the summer of his fifteenth year, the great Ole Bull came to call. Ole Bull came galloping at full speed down the road, riding a famous Arabian horse. He pulled up the horse in front of the Grieg house, leaped down, and came striding up to the door.

Edvard had heard so many tales of Ole Bull, and these tales were all so extravagant, so like the things that happen only in books, that it was a shock to see him a real man like other men.

Ole Bull sat down in the largest chair. Words flowed out of him. "I rejoice to be home," he said. "My heart is here. All the time that I am away, I long for Norway. There is no other place that has so much splendor. But let me tell you of the United States. I have just come from there, you know. It is a great land, I can tell you, so big and so interesting. The people are genial and warmhearted. My fiddle and I gave concerts all across the country to the Mississippi Valley, and then west to the gold coast. They receive one well. They cannot do enough for musicians and artists."

At this point in his talk, Ole stopped and turned to Edvard. "I have heard," he said, "that you play and compose. It would give me great pleasure if I could hear some of what you have done. Will you play for me, please?"

Edvard was afraid to play for the famous man, but Ole Bull would not be denied. "Let us hear something," he said, "something of your own composing, something that has good Norwegian sounds in it."

There was nothing that Edvard could do but play. After the first moments of awkwardness and hesitation, he forgot himself in the music, and played well with an individual, delicate, yet vigorous manner.

As Ole listened, he was at first interested, then astonished. He had heard of the talent of Edvard Grieg, but he had not expected to hear music such as this. It was a boy's music, immature and rambling. Yet there was certainly the promise of much more. There was something new in it, something original, bold, and Norwegian that Ole had not heard anywhere before. There was the lyric quality that Ole put in his own violin playing, and there was a poetic mood that was sweet and subtly compelling. As Edvard finished, Ole Bull sprang up and went to him and embraced him.

"Edvard Grieg," he said. "I have been hoping for such a one as you. I see clearly that you are to be one of our Norwegian artists. You have great talent. You must study and work hard to know music. You must play and compose. For this, there is only one thing to do. You must go where there are the best schools and teachers. You must go to Leipsig in Germany and enter the conservatory there as a student."

146

Edvard stammered. He felt wonderfully hot, and confused, and excited at the words of Ole Bull. Ole continued to smile and pour out words.

He clapped Edvard's shoulder, and Edvard felt that a fairy-tale figure was showing him the world, opening doors, pointing out a way, and that this way was what he now most desired and had not yet thought of asking for himself.

Ole Bull sat down and talked with Edvard's parents. Each of them rejoiced at his words. For Fru Grieg, the words of the famous man were like a confirmation of all that she had most ardently longed for. Soon all the plans were made. Edvard would go soon to the conservatory at Leipsig to study.

"Any other course is unthinkable," said the great Ole Bull. "It would be a crime against Mother Norway."

After Ole Bull had been gone for some time, Edvard went to the piano and sat improvising. At first his fingers rambled, and the music was vague and wandering, though with a certain sweetness. But as his mind grew quieter, music took hold of him. Slowly it grew, developing in form, in elegance, and character. It changed abruptly from major to minor, and this change had an effect like the contrast between the sternness of Norway's mountains and the tender beauty of the forests. There appeared in it, from time to time, the dissonant chords that had fascinated Edvard when he was only five years old.

Fru Grieg, listening in the next room, was moved and charmed by the playing. The chords which, through the years, she had come to love because they expressed the character of her gifted son, seemed to be full of longing. "Edvard is growing up and reaching out," she thought. "He must have opportunities to go as far as his talents can take him."

As she sat listening and feeling the power of the music, she realized with awe and thrilled surprise that Edvard's talents could well take him into the company of the great musicians of the world. Fru Grieg bowed her head in thankfulness and admiration.

CHAPTER 4

LEIPSIG

In Leipsig, Edvard was homesick. Fifteen is an early age to go out alone to a foreign country where a different language is spoken, and where the customs are different. He had come into Leipsig on a gray morning, brought by a friend of his father. Most people who see Leipsig for the first time find it fascinating. It is a city built in medieval times. The streets are narrow and winding, the houses high and set close together. Most of the roofs are gabled, and it is under these gabled roofs that the students live. At night, when the lamps are lighted, they can be seen sitting at their tables and reading the piles of books.

Grieg had one of these gabled rooms, and on the first day of homesickness, after his father's friend had gone, he sat by the window and could not keep from crying as he looked at the foreign scene. There was nothing familiar about it, nothing at all to remind him of Norway. The houses looked dark and goblinlike, and the people in the streets below were all strange. He cried without stopping until the owner of the house came to call him for the midday meal. This man tried to comfort Grieg.

"Ah, dear Herr Grieg," he said. "We are good people

149

here. Soon you will feel happy and at home. And do you not see, we have the same sun, and the same moon, and the same good God here that you have at home."

But the well-meant words could not make up for Edvard's father's friend who was now gone, and who was the last link with family and home.

Several days passed before Edvard began to yield to the kindness of his hosts, the German family, and to the charm of old Leipsig. He got over his homesickness and turned his thoughts to the music classes. In the matter of these classes, he was also very childlike. He dreamed about them, and, in his dreams, all things were wonderfully simple. He had only to go, and the miracle would begin. He would become at once a musician, a wizard in the kingdom of sound. The first classes were with Louis Plaidy. Louis Plaidy was a teacher of piano, and for Grieg, his classes were all tiresome, dry, and boring. Plaidy was a short, fat, bald man who held his finger behind his ear in order to hear the more clearly. At the first lesson, Edvard expected to hear melodies like those of Ole Bull, something new and enlivening to begin the new life in Leipsig. But Louis Plaidy was dry as dust.

"Sit down, Herr Grieg," he said in a flat tone. "So you come from Norway! Here in Germany we learn that discipline is important. We begin with exercises for the fingers. Day after day with the exercises, and we build up a technique. Begin now, please, with these exercises."

As Edvard played, Louis Plaidy said over and over: "Slow—firm—lift your fingers. Slow—firm—lift your fingers."

How desperately dull Plaidy was! At first, Edvard

thought that the exercises could not go on for more than a few minutes, but there was no sign of anything else. "Slow —firm—lift the fingers. Slow—firm—lift the fingers." Old Plaidy's right ear, held forward, did not miss the slightest suggestion of weakness.

"Herr Grieg, Herr Grieg, watch now. Slow—firm—lift the fingers. It is discipline that is important."

A few days later, Plaidy assigned a sonata by Clementi. This sonata was repulsive to Grieg, and he had difficulty keeping his mind on it when he practiced. When the lesson came, he bungled it badly. Plaidy suddenly snatched the book from the piano and pitched it in a great curve to the farthest corner of the room. "Go home and practice," he thundered. And that was all for that day.

There was one teacher who had great sympathy for Grieg. He was called Moritz Hauptmann, and he was very different from fat Plaidy. This Hauptmann taught composition. His methods were free, not bound by precise rules. "Dear Herr Grieg," he often said, "rules are important, yes, of course. But rules are not stiff, tiresome things made up by man. No, they are Nature's laws, and in nature, things are not tiresome, but rather lively and changing, and of marvelous variety.

"Discover Nature's laws, dear Herr Grieg," Hauptmann was always saying. "Many of them are printed in the textbooks, that is of course true; but if you hear strange harmonies that cannot be built by book rules, perhaps it is because the rule is not yet found by man. Continue to compose, Herr Grieg. What you are trying out, I think, may be bold and very musical."

Moritz Hauptmann was an old man and he no longer

went to the school to give his lessons. Instead he had his pupils come to his house. Grieg liked to go to his house. It was a large old residence and had splendid memories. It had been at one time the home of the famous musician, Sebastian Bach. Hauptmann always met Grieg at his door.

"Good day, my dear boy," he said smiling. "Come in, come in."

The old man wore dressing gown and slippers, and he took quantities of yellow-brown snuff. The snuff was always dripping out, and old Hauptmann was never quick enough to catch it. As Grieg came in and gave him the copybooks in which he had written his composition for the week, Hauptmann read the exercises with the greatest interest. "Yes, yes," he said nodding, "that must sound fine. Let me hear it."

Grieg sat down to play, and when he had finished, old Hauptmann smiled with pleasure. "Very good, very good," he said. "Now, that is what I call musical piano playing."

Usually Grieg played for Hauptmann far beyond the time set aside for the lesson hour. The old house that Bach had lived in echoed with a new kind of music, northern harmonies and lyrical chords and melodies. This music with the air of youth and freshness about it delighted old Hauptmann.

"Go on, go on in this direction, Herr Grieg," he said. "Do not let German teaching and our German insistence on rules push you into a stiff pattern."

Grieg improvised for the lovable warmhearted old man. The light melodies filled the old house with a springtime atmosphere. There were lovely clear runs that had become precise and perfect, strengthened by the dull work with

152

Plaidy. There were also in the music the chords that Edvard had loved as a small boy, and they still had the old interesting quality, a harmony and discord together. Often the lamps were lit at Hauptmann's old house, and Grieg would still be sitting before the big piano, the lamps lighting the piano keys and his flying fingers. Then the two would take Grieg's copybook and take one more look at the composition lesson.

"Here, I think you must do better," the old man said. "Do you agree?"

Edvard nodded and resolved to go home at once and improve the dull line. When Hauptmann, at last, shuffled to the door in his slippers and put a last pinch of the yellow-brown snuff in his nose, he never failed to send Grieg off with encouraging words.

"Go in your own direction," he said. "It is new and musical, and I think of great promise."

Grieg had other teachers and he worked for most of them conscientiously and well. Yet, all of the time, it was only with the one teacher, Hauptmann, that he felt free and happy. The German insistence on rules, the old forms and conventional harmonies, was never sympathetic to him. Sometimes he felt smothered as though he must escape at once to Norway, and at these times he felt that all the time at the Conservatory was a waste for him, like a desert. One good thing was that he heard a great deal of good music, Schumann, and Mozart, and the new composer, Richard Wagner. Grieg heard *Tannhauser* by this new composer fourteen times and found it wonderfully stimulating, different, and upsetting.

The four school years passed, and Grieg progressed in

skill and knowledge. At the end of the second year, when he was seventeen, he was ill with a serious lung inflammation. Because of this illness, he had only one lung to breathe with for the rest of his life. Nevertheless, after he recovered, he learned to manage and continued to work hard. He was never satisfied with his studies at the conservatory. Later when he desired to compose large works and found himself unequal to the task, he thought that his training had not been thorough or complete. But he learned much more than he knew or ever recognized. His school notebooks today are in a museum in Bergen, and these notebooks show how conscientiously he worked.

Probably one trouble was that he was very young, a Norwegian boy from a land newly independent from Denmark. He often said later, "We Norwegians grow up slowly." When one is young, it is natural to sit back, to be a timid student, unsure of what to take from the world. It is later that one sees all the riches and all the wonders.

But of course Grieg could not know the main cause of his dissatisfaction with the German school. This was that he would soon become Norway's first great composer. He would be the first to express in music the spirit of the northern land and the northern people. Before he could make this great gift to the world, he had to find a new way, new harmonies, and new methods. He had learned the technique of the German masters, but this technique was for a different kind of music. And so he felt baffled and unhappy.

CHAPTER 5

GRIEG MEETS A RED-HAIRED MAN

It is a rare thing that a young artist can go directly and without hesitation to the work that he wants to do. It is usually necessary to begin to work before one sees clearly; to try one way of doing things, and then another, and another, and another.

It was this way with Edvard Grieg. After Leipsig, he came home to Bergen. He gave a concert in his home town and earned some money so that he could buy scores of musical compositions to study. He managed some compositions that were good. Very soon, however, he saw that he was not yet ready for important work. He must have further experiences, further exploring.

And so, after a year in Bergen, he went out in the world again. This time he went to Copenhagen in Denmark, and it was here that the important adventures began.

Copenhagen is an old European city. It is a city of theaters, and book and music shops. It is a city where many concerts are given, where artists sit talking in the many cafés about life, and books, and what is happening out in the world. For many years it had been the capital of the northern nations, Norway, Sweden, and Denmark, and had long been a center of activity. For a young man like Grieg, after the winter of quiet, it was exciting and stimulating. He plunged into the city life. He took a room in an old house and set up his books, papers, and pencils. He ate in the cafés, listened to the lively talk, and could not have enough of it. He made friends, and one day met Copenhagen's most famous citizen, tall, homely, lovable Hans Christian Andersen.

Then suddenly the thing happened which pushed him into his great work. At the end of a beautiful autumn day, Grieg came into the old Tivoli restaurant for his supper. He had no sooner seated himself at a table than a young man came up. This young man had flaming red hair, freckles, a wide merry smile, and a voice so warm and young that it was like sunshine on a spring day.

"You are Edvard Grieg, and I am Rikard Nordraak," the young man said. "At last we meet, we two great men!" Nordraak laughed. "It's true, you know. I know some of your songs. I am a composer too. I am also a poet and a singer and an actor. May I sit down? We can eat herring together."

"Of course," said Grieg. "I also know of you."

The young man with the red hair now took charge. "I was serious in what I said. I am a Norwegian, as you know. I love our land, wonderful fierce Glittertind with her snow crown; Trondheim, a city of viking times; the fjords, the waterfalls, the thousand streams! It's poetry, the stuff dreams are made on."

Nordraak stopped for a moment, grinned, and then became serious. "Edvard Grieg, listen to me. I said I knew your music. What I want to say is this. It is very impor-

156

tant and you must allow me to say it. I see in your music what you can do. You must get Norway into your music, Edvard Grieg. You must write down our dreams and our strangeness, trolls, spirits, Thor and Freya, thunderbolts in the mountains, northern lights, and our long days like twilight. That is what has not been done before, and that is what you must do, Edvard Grieg."

Nordraak stopped for a moment. He drank coffee and began again. "Oh, let me talk," he cried. "Here we two are at last. We must make ourselves interesting. I am full of talk. We will order coffee and more coffee and talk of Norway. You studied in Leipsig, and I in Berlin, but all the time that I studied, I also read Wergeland and Bjornson. Do you know them well? They are great writers of Norway."

"Yes," said Grieg, "I also have read Wergeland and I have heard Ole Bull talk of him. They are both good Norwegians."

"Ole Bull is a great man," answered Nordraak quickly, "and Wergeland is a great man, but you and I can go much farther. They opened the doors for us. We are here at the right time, and dear Grieg, both of us have the necessary genius."

Nordraak laughed. "I am serious," he said. "I am full of plans, stuffed like a barrel. Plans for operas, plays, symphonies. Pull out the bung, and they will come flowing."

"I am more slow," answered Grieg. "I feel my way. Thoughts whisper in me for a while, then they grow."

"I know," laughed Nordraak. "In that you are more northern than I." As Nordraak talked, his smile and con-

157

fidence were so contagious, so merry, good-humored, and exuberant, that Grieg was carried away.

"Can we get all those things that you talk of in music?" he said.

"The trolls take us if we can't," said Nordraak. "Just now, Edvard Grieg, you are writing too much in the German manner. Put aside the music of Germany. It is not for us. Those chords you sometimes use—those queer ones, like the sounds of smothered glaciers—you must do more with them. And those very delicate soft melodies of yours like the morning mood of our mountain land—go in that way, dear Edvard Grieg. The word, *northern, northern, northern,* must be always in your head." Nordraak stopped. "Let me get my breath," he said, "and I can go on forever. Words are good, talk is good. One is kindled by good talk. Let us build up a world of Norway with our words, and dream ourselves into a Norwegian, Norwegian future."

As Nordraak talked, Edvard Grieg felt as though this red-haired young man were his closest and dearest friend. It was as though they had known each other all of their lives. The blithe talk was like a sharp medicine that he needed to wake up from dreaminess, from uncertainty, from groping in the fog of what-to-do, how-to-do-it, how-to-begin. He had always thought of himself as a student, as a humble onlooker at important people and scenes. And now here was this redhead, pushing, persuading, pointing out the way ahead with certainty.

"Come, let us go," Nordraak said at last. "I must see where you live, see your piano and your books, where you work."

They went together through the streets and came to the rooms that Grieg had taken. "Come in," said Grieg. "This is where I stay."

Nordraak looked around with interest. "I like it very much," he said. "It is a good hideaway. There are your papers, and the piano is a good one, I see. Let me try it out with some songs I have made. The words are from Bjornson, his peasant stories."

Nordraak began to play. The songs were full of spirit, simple, melodious, appealing.

"Bravo!" said Grieg when he had finished. "It is full of life, a real gust of the Norwegian spirit."

Nordraak turned from the piano. "Let me play you a new thing of mine, something more important. The words are also by Bjornson." This time Nordraak was more serious. The music was firm and stirring, and Bjornson's words which told of Norway and its history were beautiful. The lamplight fell directly on Nordraak and his flame-red hair. The appearance of the young musician, the compelling music, and the poetic words of Bjornson, each in its own way was striking. Grieg saw that Nordraak put all of his love for Norway into the words as he sang.

> "Yes, we love this land that towers
> Where the ocean foams
> Storm-swept it embowers
> Many thousand homes."

When Nordraak finished, for once, he was quiet. It was as though the words and the music said all that he wished to say about his land.

Grieg was equally moved. "It is beautiful," he said after

a few minutes of silence. "How well Norway is described! That is the way I think of our country, as the land that towers. The music is excellent and fits the words."

The two young men sitting there in the lamplight talked longer of the song. They did not know that soon a great honor would come to it. It would be chosen as the national anthem of Norway. All over the country, the Norwegian people would sing it and come to love both Nordraak's music and the beautiful words, "Yes, we love this land that towers."

After that night, Nordraak and Grieg were constantly together. Nordraak knew all the old Norwegian fairy tales and folk lore, all the stirring incidents of Norway's history. He was full of plans for symphonies and operas based on these stories, and he sketched them out for Grieg with delight and enthusiasm.

"Edvard Grieg," he would say, speaking in the most fascinated, serious way, "put all of it into music. It will be incomparable, and so beautiful that all the world will love Norway."

As the days in Copenhagen passed, Grieg's way became more clear, and he worked fruitfully. His songs began to lose their ordered Danish grace and German restraint, and take on a new quality that was like the spirit of his northern land. When, within a short time, he composed a group of songs, he took them to Nordraak and dedicated them to him. Nordraak played them one night and then sprang up and embraced his friend.

"Yes," he shouted, "I worship such songs. The music is as if I had written it myself."

When the two friends were separated, they wrote letters, and in these letters, Nordraak continued to encourage Grieg. Once he wrote from Berlin: "I feel so clearly that now great things in music are approaching. . . . How glad I am to have met *at last* one in whom I put such firm faith and hope."

Grieg read and reread many times the inspiring words. "We Norwegian grow up slowly," he thought. "The trolls take me, I'm slower than most. There is no telling how much more slow I might have been without Nordraak. My feeling for our great melancholy Westland country, from the days of childhood, has been intense, but without Nordraak, I might never have known that to express it was my work."

As the days of the summer passed, Grieg continued to work well. He and Nordraak were so full of plans that even in two lifetimes, there would be too little time for their working out.

Then, so quickly that Grieg could not believe it, Nordraak became ill. The doctor in charge said that he had consumption. But when Grieg went to see him, he could not believe it. Nordraak appeared as he always had, eyes alight with interest, his smile as merry and engaging. The only difference was that he tired quickly, and talked, after a while, with difficulty and a new harsh breathlessness. Yet there was the same confidence in the work they would do together, the same inspiring belief in it.

"It is we Norwegians who know the fresh air of the mountains," Nordraak grinned, "who will give the music of the future to the world." Nordraak laughed, then caught his breath, and Grieg could not endure seeing it.

In November, Grieg had to leave his friend to conduct

a concert in Leipsig. He had to get on with his work. He traveled some in Germany and Italy, studying and playing. Perhaps he did not know how fast life was running out for his friend. He had one letter which should have told him. At the end were these lines:

"Now, you must come, Grieg. Don't delay any longer—I must have you again. Write immediately when you receive these lines to say that you are coming at once to your devoted

"Rikard Nordraak"

But Grieg delayed too long, and Rikard Nordraak died without having had Grieg again. We can imagine what Grieg felt when the friend dearest and closest to his heart was taken from him. He put some of this feeling in music, in a stormy requiem march of mourning which he called *Funeral March for Rikard Nordraak*. Of all the compositions that Grieg would write to the end of his life this would be one of his favorites. He always carried it with him and requested that it be used also for his own funeral march.

Nordraak had died in Berlin. The winter passed and spring came again before Grieg visited the grave. He went alone. The place was beautiful and open, and looked out to the city. Grieg sat for a while, finding it impossible to think of Nordraak gone. There were oak trees standing near Nordraak's grave, and as Grieg looked, the sun on the new small leaves glistened. Grieg picked several of the leaves and turned them over slowly in his hands.

"Rikard Nordraak," he thought, "you put everyone whom you met in a creative springtime. You were the great one, I the follower, the struggler, the wrestler with trolls. Your idea was great and true, and it must endure. I must work it out for both of us."

That night Grieg wrote to Nordraak's father. He enclosed in the letter one of the shining oak leaves from the tree near Rikard's grave.

Now Grieg entered a new period of his life. His student days were over, and his *wanderjahr*, his first free time out in the world. It was time to go home, to get on with work, to give evidence of his faith in the national ideals called to life by his friend, Rikard Nordraak.

"The trolls take me," thought Grieg. "Time passes. I must put away dreams and get on. No big work is yet done."

CHAPTER 6

A GREAT WORK

Winter in Norway! Cold and wind and the big snows!
The country and fjord valleys were goblin lands. The
waterfalls were icicle stalactites. And Oslo, the capital
city, was a northland capital where the people wore great-
coats, mufflers, galoshes, and furs. By midafternoon, the
winter evening had begun and the lamps were lighted.
People fled inside, the coffee shops filled up, and the piles
of sweet pastry disappeared.

Grieg was one of this Oslo throng. He gave some concerts and many piano lessons, and he tried to compose. It
was a harsh and cold time for him, and he was learning of
the difficulties of the artist's way in a country where the
arts of the land are at their beginning. When he came
home from a concert that he had conducted, he threw his
cape coat on the chair and exclaimed wearily: "How the
people jabber! Anyone who wishes to hear music might
as well stay home." Then he would sit down at his table,
eat bread and yellow cheese. After he had eaten, he felt
some better, but still bruised, beaten down by the indif-
ferent jabbering audience.

"How does one get on?" he thought. "What is the good

of making music if no one will listen? It would be better to be a troll on a mountaintop and squeak to the other trolls."

So the winter went. Hours of work, conducting, and lessons. And there were only the leftover fragments of hours for the work that was nearest to his heart, the composing. It was a bad time, a jog-trot time, a time to get over and forget. Grieg scurried before the wind, and at the end of the gray afternoon, hurried in with the others to take pastries and chocolate. He looked very young with his blond hair like a mane, brushed back from his face. His blue eyes were always dreamy. He looked appealing and attractive, a little odd in his shortness and quickness.

But the snows go, and the spring comes, and this particular spring for Grieg would be one of the best in his whole life. First, he married his cousin, Nina Hagerup. This little Nina was a singer, the daughter of an actress. She sang with great charm, as though she were telling a story. She was about as tall as Grieg, and she was droll, merry, and full of life. They went together for the summer vacation to a small country town near Copenhagen. In any northern land, where winter is long, and the snow and ice and bitter winds drive the people to live indoors, summer comes like a liberation. The earth turns freshly green, the air is soft, and the little summer winds push one off to the gardens or woodlands. By the first of June, Grieg and Nina were settled in a two-room cottage, a gardener's little house.

"It's like a palace for a mouse," Nina laughed.

They took long walks through the beautiful Danish countryside and felt the summer go into them. Grieg began to spend long hours at the piano. He always worked into the mood of composing, first playing a little, exploring, trying a melody and warming up to it. Soon he would be thumping like a madman, smashing through into the world of music. *Thump, thump,* away with the world! Away with Oslo and the long hours of music lessons! Away with the hours of depression, and doubt, and searching! Back to the mountains and mountain lakes so blue and shining! To mountain springs and flowering valleys! To waterfalls noble and playful! Back to Nordraak and the good hours of confident dreaming. Nina, seeing how things were with Grieg at such moments, slipped out of the little house and left him undisturbed in his world of harmony.

When, after many days, all the thumping had resolved itself into music, the composition that came out of it was a concerto for piano with orchestra. Grieg called it *Piano Concerto in A Minor, Opus 16.* It is a wonderful work. It is now famous all over the world, and nearly all concert pianists like to play it. One Norwegian critic wrote that the beautiful concerto contained nature impressions of all Norway, and that one part, which is called the *Adagio,* was like a lonely mountain tarn, circled by mountains, which lies dreaming. An English critic much later wrote also of this *Adagio.* He spoke of its "long-drawn sweetness," and said that it reminded him of Tennyson's line of poetry, "Dark and true and tender is the North."

When Grieg finished writing down the beautiful piano concerto, he was elated and knew that he had written a masterpiece. He played it for Nina in the long summer twilight, and the gardener's cottage was filled with music. Near the end, where there is a tremendous scale which

166

covers all the piano, Grieg played with fiery energy and mounting excitement. Here it was, a great work, a new creation, a magnificent concerto, northern in spirit, one of the first great works of art to come out of Norway.

At the end of the year, when Grieg was again working in Oslo, another wonderful thing happened which helped him along in his career. He received a letter from the most famous musician of the time, Franz Liszt.

Franz Liszt was a composer and a concert pianist, and had such a dramatic, commanding personality that he was like an emperor in the kingdom of music. He had lately become a Catholic, and now, wearing the long robes of a Catholic abbé, he was more than ever striking to look at. He had white hair that he wore to his shoulders; he was tall and carried himself erectly. When he played, his hands tossed and swooped over the keyboard like swift birds. It was no wonder that Grieg was excited to have the letter from the famous man. It was written from Italy, from a monastery where Liszt was then staying. These are the words of the letter:

> "Monsieur—it gives me great pleasure to tell you that I have just seen a sonta of yours, *Opus 8*. I must tell you that it shows a strong talent for composition, a talent that is original and inventive, and which, I think, will rise to high rank. I hope that we may soon become acquainted. Please accept, monsieur, my esteem and most sincere good wishes.
>
> "Franz Liszt"

Grieg ran gleefully with it to Nina, and they read and

reread the hearty words. "I can put the letter to good use," Grieg said at once. "It is more than just encouragement to me. I shall apply to the government for money from the traveling fund for artists. With this letter from the great Franz Liszt, perhaps the officials will think I am worth helping out a bit. Then we could go to Italy, get out into the world. I can refresh my mind, get new impressions, and find time and peace for composing."

"It is what must happen," Nina said seriously. "You must hear music, and talk music, and meet people like Liszt. You must grow strong for bouts with the Norwegian spirits. I have been more than ever sure of it since the piano concerto."

Grieg wrote the letter of application to the government, and enclosed the letter from Liszt. Within a short time the request was granted, and the wonderful trip to the south-land was planned. They set out gaily, these two little Norwegians. They were going to a warm and sunny land, a land sought out by artists because it had long encouraged the arts of painting, and singing, and music making.

"Hurrah for the future!" Grieg said as he settled their things in the train.

Nina laughed. "Your music will be music of the future," she said confidently.

How to describe Rome and the impressions of it that Edvard Grieg and Nina had! After Norway, the city itself was like a great treasure house, a museum filled with the beautiful and noble buildings of the past. They wandered among the monuments, marvelling at the work done by artists of many generations. Paintings, sculpture, the ancient and vast libraries, the enormous Coliseum where Ole Bull had once played, the classic public buildings. All were magnificent and thrilling to the young artists from the young country of the North. There was singing in the streets and shops, and it was good singing. The songs were from the great Italian operas. This love of music and knowledge of music that was in most of the people and was so evident everywhere that one went in Italy, was wonderful to Grieg and Nina.

"Someday," Nina said, "we will have great Norwegian music, and someday, after we have concerts and symphonies, many of them in all our cities, Norwegians too will sing and know music as the Italians do."

One day in February, after Grieg and Nina had been enjoying the bright winter days for some weeks, the message came that they had dreamed of many times. It was from Franz Liszt, and it invited Grieg to call to see him at the monastery where he stayed when he was in town. A Danish friend was with Grieg when the message came. "It's a great honor," he said, speaking with excitement. "You must take something to show him. What have you? Be certain to take something he will like."

"But I have nothing," Grieg said in dismay. "Everything is at home in Norway."

"Find something then," said the friend firmly. "He will expect it, and you cannot disappoint him."

Grieg then remembered that he had earlier given a copy of a sonata of his to another friend. "I gave away a copy of my sonata a few days ago," he said. "I'll have to play 'giver—giver—taker-back.'" He rushed off in a breathless hurry, and soon was back with the sonata. "I have also *Nordraak's Funeral March*," he said, "and a few songs."

He went off alone the next morning, down the sunlit streets. The music was in a roll under his arm. He walked so fast that he was soon out of breath. When he came to the monastery, the sunlight was a mellow gold on the old stones. So this was where he would meet Franz Liszt! It was fitting that the first meeting take place in so splendid a place. While he marvelled at the rambling monastery and at the wonderful fact that he was really here and about to meet Franz Liszt, a gate in the wall opened, and Grieg found himself ushered into the huge central hall of the monastery.

In a moment, Liszt came. He walked quickly and smiled in the most genial way. "I am glad to see you at last, Herr Grieg," he said heartily. "We have corresponded, have we not?"

"Your letter brought me here," Grieg answered. Then he told the story of how he had used the letter, sending it to the government office when he applied for the artist's fellowship.

Liszt let out a roar of laughter. "That is good, good," he said, speaking in German. *"Sehr schön, sehr schön."* As he spoke, he saw the roll of music under Grieg's arm. At once his long fingers reached out for the pages. Grieg hurried to open the package, and Liszt began to read the pages of the music rapidly just as though he were reading a story. As he read, he nodded and smiled. At last he called out heartily, "Bravo, bravo! Good, good, *sehr schön, sehr schön.*"

Grieg's spirits began to soar. Liszt, still holding fast to the music, walked toward a beautiful grand piano which

170

was at the end of the monastery hall. "Come, come, you must play it for me," he said.

"No, I cannot do it well," Grieg answered. "I will make a mess of it. The sonata is newly composed, and I have not practiced it."

"No matter," said Liszt, "I must hear it. You must try it." He spoke with so much enthusiasm and interest that Grieg saw that he could do nothing else but play. He sat down at the beautiful grand piano and began. In a few minutes, Liszt was nodding his head. "Ah, how full of life! Now, let me tell you, that pleases me. Once again, please."

Further on in the sonata, where Grieg had written a violin part above the piano music, Liszt sat down at the side of his guest and played this violin part. He played beautifully with such singing quality that Grieg smiled with delight. "Good, good," said Liszt. Soon there came a fast movement of the sonata, and Liszt continued to play the violin part; the two, the old musician and the young one dashing along, both getting more and more in form. They ended in a burst of flying notes.

"Bravo, bravo!" Liszt called out as he jumped up. "But we must have more. We cannot stop there."

Grieg felt happiness soaring up inside him like a great wave. "I have a minuet for the piano," he said, speaking with difficulty because of his emotion.

Liszt nodded, walked rapidly around the piano, his abbé's robes sweeping out after him. Grieg began the charming melody. He had chosen it because of its Norwegian quality, thinking that the national character of the music would be new and interesting. After the first lines, Liszt began to sing the melody as Grieg played. He did this with great feeling and power, striding back and forth, nodding his head all at the same time. Grieg was quite carried away. He played his own music brilliantly, with vigor and yet with an appealing youthful charm, and it was clear that he had won the heart of the great Franz Liszt. When it was over, and Liszt had expressed his delight, Grieg dared to make a request.

"Can I hear you play, sir?" he asked. "You cannot let me leave the South without hearing something from you."

Liszt shrugged his shoulders and laughed. "No, I am not like that," he said. "I'll play what you wish."

With a flourish, he pulled out a score that he had just completed and began to set the keys in motion. His long fingers appeared to fly over the keys, bringing out a mass of fire and fervor. As Grieg listened and watched, he thought: "He is like a prophet announcing the Day of Judgment. All the spirits of the universe are quarreling under his fingers."

When Liszt had finished, he stood up and said quite casually, as though he had done nothing at all, or as though the magnificent torrent of sound was something that one could hear every day, "Well, now that you have heard some of my work, let us go further into your sonata."

Grieg was embarrassed. "No," he said, "not after that, I shouldn't like to."

"But why not? Give it here. I will do it."

And Liszt took up Grieg's music which he had not before seen and began to play it. Grieg stared. The abbé was all over the piano, not a note was missed. Grieg marvelled to hear his own music, for here it was full and rich, played

172

with genius and with a majestic beauty. When Liszt had finished, Grieg laughed in elation and stammered out his admiration.

The abbé only smiled. "You could expect that from me. I'm an old experienced musician, you know."

But Grieg still could not get over it. Liszt would have him play a little more, and this time Grieg played the *Funeral March for Nordraak*. This was also to the taste of Liszt, and when at last Grieg went home, he felt hot in the head and knew that he had just spent two of the most interesting hours of his life.

Two months later, there was a second meeting with Liszt which went as wonderfully well as the first. Fortunately Grieg had just received from his publisher in Germany the manuscript of his piano concerto. He took this with him. He was anxious to show it and to see what Liszt would say of it. When he came to the monastery, he found quite a crowd of friends with Liszt, and the abbé appeared to be in excellent spirits. The abbé, as on the first visit, greeted Grieg cordially and again seeing the roll of music beneath his arm, reached out his long spiderlike fingers for it.

Grieg handed it to him. He thought Liszt would read the music through, but, because of the technical difficulties, he did not think it would be possible for him to play the concerto at sight.

Liszt turned to Grieg. "Will you play?" he asked.

"No," answered Grieg, "I cannot. I haven't practiced it sufficiently."

Liszt smiled. "Well then," he said, "I will show you that I also cannot."

Liszt sat down at the piano and began to play. He took the beginning too fast, but after Grieg indicated the tempo, the concerto came out, precise, clear, and thrilling to hear. Its northern quality, strange and fresh, and dreamlike, deeply affected the small audience of music lovers. And at the end, where there was the climax, the grand fortissimo, which was a tremendous scale covering all of the piano keys, Liszt stopped suddenly. He stood up and left the piano, and holding up his arms in a theatric gesture, he walked in great strides down the monastery hall. As he walked, he sang, roaring out the theme. When he came to the end, he stretched out his arm commandingly like an emperor and shouted: "G, G, not G sharp! Famous! That's the real Swedish banko!" Then he strode back to the piano, repeated the tremendous scale, nodding his head and singing, and finished it off. This time, when he rose, he turned to Grieg and handed the concerto back to him. Then he spoke with great cordiality: "Go on boldly, I tell you. You have the talent. Do not let anyone hold you back."

Grieg hurried out, the piano concerto again rolled under his arm, with the bold inspiring words of Liszt going around in his head. Later, he wrote to the Norwegian government telling of the time with Liszt. "I shall be more than ever the musician of the north," he wrote. "Liszt encouraged me greatly in this northernness. It was the national element in my composition that roused him to enthusiasm."

CHAPTER 7

A LETTER FROM IBSEN

One morning in January when Nina and Grieg were back
again in Oslo, an important letter came. It was from Henrik
Ibsen, the most famous writer of Norway. Ibsen had written a wonderful play called *Peer Gynt*.

Grieg was surprised to have a letter from the famous
man. He read:

"Dear Mr. Grieg,

"I send you these lines because of a plan I wish to
carry out. . . . I intend to arrange *Peer Gynt* . . .
for performance on the stage. Will you write the required music? . . . The second act must be treated
musically as the composer sees fit, but the devil must
be at large in it. . . . I beg of you to let me know if
you are willing to undertake this work. . . . Let me
have your answer as soon as possible.

"Your devoted friend,
"Henrik Ibsen"

Grieg looked at Nina. Here was something to set the
imagination on fire! "It is a great honor," he said, speaking with excitement. "Of course the devil must be at large

in it, a whole pack of devils. It must also be full of something else, a thick, tough, stubborn, troll-like Norwegianness. But can I get it? I long to do it if it would come."

As Grieg sat holding the letter and reading again the tempting offer, the morning sunlight glinted over him. He looked just the person to write the music for Ibsen's fantasy. He appeared sympathetic, original, droll, with eyes very blue and Norwegian, blond unruly hair standing out from his face, and with one leg crossed over the other, so that he looked small and doubled up.

After breakfast, Grieg and Nina put on their coats and hats. Grieg put his umbrella under his arm in case the weather should change. Then they walked down the main street of Oslo and talked of the play.

"Of course you can do it," said Nina confidently. "It will come. Do you know I have just thought of an old folk song. You know the lines:

" 'And this ballad has thus got a soul for itself
And comes gaily tobogganing down on a plank.' "

That is what will happen to you, Edvard. Suddenly you will have ideas. They will grow and grow until they get a soul and come gaily toboganning down on a plank."

Grieg laughed aloud. "Perhaps," he said.

The two of them enjoyed the shop windows of the city. Grieg lingered longest in front of a large delicatessen store. The windows were filled with pastries spread out in a brave display, small cakes, and tarts, and frosted rolls in a great variety of shapes. When Nina laughed at his interest, he waved his umbrella and exclaimed with enthusiasm:

"It is like a symphony. How perfect in all details, in form, in content, and harmony!"

"Let us go in then," said Nina. "Let us take some of the symphony home for lunch."

They enjoyed choosing the decorated pastries, and when they walked out of the shop, each carried a large paper bag. They continued to walk, enjoying the brisk cold air and the life of the city streets. They both felt gay and excited as though something strenuous and wonderful were just ahead of them.

That night at home, they reread *Peer Gynt*. The winter dark had come early, and the lamplight put soft shadows in the room and made the setting harmonious for the reading of Ibsen's fantasy. When at last Grieg stopped reading, there was a long silence. Both he and Nina were under the spell of the strange poem. It was difficult. Some parts were hard to understand. Yet what a world of rich fantasy it contained! Grieg knew that if he were to compose music for such a great imaginative work, the music must not fail. Witchery and wildness must be in it. The trolls must hiss and thump. There would have to be lyrical melodies, the voices of the forest, sweet, wild, and haunting.

"I'm not sure that I can do it," Grieg said aloud. "I will finish reading it tomorrow. Let the poem stay in my head a while and we shall see."

Several days passed before Grieg made up his mind. He was nervous and uncertain, not knowing whether he could get the poem into music. He took long walks alone, both in daylight and at night, thinking of *Peer Gynt*, the troll scenes, and all the queer fantasy. The play began to grow in his mind and take hold of him strongly. One night he began to talk of it again.

"I think it is for me," he said, nodding his head. "It will be frightfully difficult, tough, unmanageable, Norwegian, full of rocks and bogs. But I cannot put it down."

"Of course not," said Nina seriously. "It has such an air of 'Hi—come along!'"

Grieg laughed. "I shall answer Mr. Ibsen's letter to-morrow," he said.

It was summer before Grieg started the *Peer Gynt* music. He and Nina went to the country near Bergen. There, in the mountain and fjord country, in the kind of land that was like the land of *Peer Gynt*, Grieg hoped to work. He and Nina took long walks and renewed their knowledge of the beautiful country. One day they passed a little bungalow built high up on the top of one of the hills. There were windows on all sides of it. On one side, these windows commanded views out over the sea; and on the other, there were views of the towering mountains. Grieg looked at the bungalow, and at once he knew that if he could only have this little house with its wide, grand *Peer Gynt* views, he could begin.

"Oh, the luck to be allowed to work in such a place!" he said. "No man would come here. I could live in my thoughts with the troll pack and the mountain king. I think I could get them in music."

Grieg found the owner of the bungalow, and in a few days all the arrangements were made. A piano was carried up the steep hill and set in the little mountain house. The papers and pencils were made ready. On the night when all this was completed, Grieg was excited, filled with enthusiasm.

"I am like a madman," he said to Nina. "I must begin. I am longing like a child."

He went up alone the next morning, and the summer sunlight was brilliant on the sea below him, so that the water was truly a soft Norwegian blue, glinting and twinkling. The mountains were close, and so clearly to be seen that he imagined that he could see the stiff-jumping mountain goats. When he came into the little many-windowed house, it was flooded with this clear light, and the wonderful views were like a part of it. Soon he was sitting at the piano, thumping like mad.

It is not strange that the melodies that he wrote in those first days were delicate and clear, because the mood of the morning mountain wonderland went into the songs. All creation is difficult. So much must go into it, not thinking only, but thinking that has with it strong feeling and lively imagining. Grieg imagined the Ibsen scenes, saw them clearly, and felt the mood and spirit of each. And so, slowly, slowly, working through each long light summer day, he was able to write most of the melodies for the play. The first to be written was the first *Solveig's Song*. This song later became so widely loved and sung that now both the melody and the words are well known.

In the bright summer evening, when Nina sang it for the first time, both she and Grieg were thrilled by it. In the years to come, whenever they heard it, they thought of the delight that the first singing had given them. Once, one summer when they were visiting in an isolated mountain hotel, they had an odd experience. At twilight, a group of peasants from the surrounding mountains, came in carrying zithers. They had heard that the composer, Grieg, was at their small hotel. They played *Solveig's Song* on their zithers, and the music, so unexpected and appealing, stirred Grieg so strangely that he turned pale.

"Can you understand it?" he said, turning to Nina. "It's more than I deserve."

Besides the lovely *Solveig's Song,* four other melodies from the *Peer Gynt* music are especially famous. Grieg collected these, to be played together, and they are called the *First Peer Gynt Suite.*

One of these songs is called *Morning Mood.* It is possible for almost everyone to hear it now because fine records are made of it. It is like morning sunlight on the sea, with dreamlike forests and mountains all around. One writer has said of it that it is like a "vision of Paradise obtained in a dream."

Another song is called *In the Hall of the Mountain King.* It is entirely different from *Morning Mood.* It takes us to a strange, hideous scene. Peer Gynt is in the mountain king's hall where the gnomes and trolls live. He is trying to escape in pell-mell flight, but the trolls pursue, waddling, thumping, screeching. Wilder, faster, louder, madder, goes the scene, and the thumping, waddling, and screeching go on and on. The mountain king's hall resounds with the crash. But at last, in the midst of all the tumult, church bells from a distant valley begin softly to ring, and the demon scene and the demon hall collapse at the holy sound. The music ends with this resounding crash.

One can imagine Grieg writing this scene. Certainly he

saw it all before him clearly, and then began thumping at the notes, repeating them, getting down the ugly troll pack howls and fury.

The third song of the *First Peer Gynt Suite* is called *Aase's Death*. *Aase* was the mother of *Peer Gynt*. The song is written in a minor key, and is simple and sorrowful.

The fourth of the famous songs is called *Anitra's Dance*. This is a graceful airy dance with the delicate oriental air of the Bedouin's daughter, *Anitra*, whom *Peer* loved briefly when he went to Morocco. Grieg wrote later to a friend about this music: "It is a soft little dance which I am most anxious should sound delicate and beautiful, on no account must it be danced by more than a few. . . . Do please treat it like a pet child."

The summer passed for Edvard Grieg. The little mountain house had given him inspiration and quiet, the things necessary for high accomplishment. Though all of the writing of the *Peer Gynt* music would not be completed before two more years had passed, yet it was here in the mountain bungalow that the ideas were found and put down in simple melodies.

Once an old Danish friend of Nina's who often passed by his little work house, and always saw him working at the piano or writing table, said to Nina: "You must be very glad, my child, that you have such a husband; one who sits at his work from morning till night, instead of going off to the club to play cards."

Nina had smiled at the remark. It had always seemed to her to be the most natural thing in the world that Grieg should sit for long hours at his work table.

But the day came at last when he no longer sat working

over the *Peer Gynt* melodies. The great work was done, and the songs were given to the world. Ibsen's fantasy and Grieg's music were ready to take their places together among the great accomplishments of the world, to give delight forever to all people who love poetry and music.

Grieg rejoiced at the fine work done, and Nina rejoicing with him, liked to speak of the old folk song:

"And this ballad has thus got a soul for itself
And comes gaily tobogganing down on a plank."

"The music has got a soul for itself," she liked to say, "and it will go gaily and boldly out into the world."

CHAPTER 8

SUMMER IDYL

Once Grieg wrote to a friend, "I think it is the time you live in that gives you its whack." He meant that there are certain times in the life of a country when the people are adventurers, explorers, or crusaders; and other times when an age of machines comes and all the fast and curious minds want to invent and work over these machines; and at still other times, people grow tired of the machines and the restless exploring, and want to enjoy the arts such as music, and painting, and writing.

Grieg was complaining when he wrote. He was discouraged, in a low mood. It seemed to him that his time was not congenial for him, that it was a harsh time of awakening for his country, and that there were no people to understand his music. His time was getting in its whacks, molding the characters of people, but this molding was not for music. So he felt baffled, unnourished, drained of inspiration and the power to work. At such times he had to escape out into the world so that he might have contacts with musicians and with music. He went restlessly, and for a while, seeing the world and hearing music helped him. But the help was only for a short while. Soon he would find that he had to get back to Norway. He had to have his land, the mountains, the mystery, and the wildness. He had to have them even with the loneliness.

Sometimes in a great European city, he would stop in the crowd. "I must have the mountains and the lakes," he would think, "the home of wildness, and a little mouse-hole to hide myself away in."

Such a need of the north and northern spring would come to him that he could scarcely wait to return. "I long to be a troll on a mountaintop," he would say, trying to express the deep craving. "Spring is spring for me only in Norway. I must have a quiet morning in a boat among rocks and reefs with birds singing." And so he would be off to his fairy and troll-ridden land, to the isolation and the musical blankness. And again its beauty gave him what he needed.

Several summers after the *Peer Gynt* music was written, Grieg came with Nina and saw, for the first time, the Hardanger Fjord. This fjord is so beautiful that it is called by many "the smiling Hardanger." In the spring, it is like a place in fairyland. The apple and cherry trees all come into blossom, and the stern mountains are decorated with pink and white and red bouquets. The farm animals wander far afield, and the low sounds of cowbells, and the light tinkling of goat bells put music in the air. Many of the farm-houses have turf-covered roofs, and in this turf the first spring flowers bloom. On some of the houses, so many dandelions burst into bloom all at one time that the whole cottage appears merry and golden.

Grieg was elated by all the beauty. He took a small house in the village of Lofthus. From this house, he could look up to an orchard in bloom, and out across the fjord to a mountainside where there was a gleaming blue-white glacier. He wrote to a friend with enthusiasm about all the beauty and the fresh mountain air: "You couldn't help feeling well if you were here. The air is so light, one feels like a feather."

After a few days, Grieg was ready to get to work. He had had built a little house of his own to work in. The little hut was in a stand of birch trees on a hillside above the fjord, and it was dollhouse size, just big enough for a piano, a table, and chair, and fireplace, and Grieg. In the mornings after breakfast, Grieg could not wait to go to the "tune house." It appeared snug and bewitching set in the birch trees. Like the story *Peer Gynt*, it had an air of "Hi—come along." Grieg imagined that he could work there in a peaceful quiet, ruffled only by the songs of the forest birds.

But it was not long before the "come along" air of the little hut, which was so attractive to Grieg, proved to be likewise irresistible to the country people. At first he worked well, trying out his musical thoughts with boldness and freedom. But presently he began to be disturbed. He thought he heard a rustling in the grass. A few seconds later he heard it again, and then a stealthy sound of leaves being disturbed. He stood up and looked out the window. There was no longer a mystery. A crowd of country people were sitting in the grass around the "tune house." They were smiling and nodding their heads and enjoying to the utmost the forest concert. Grieg came out of the little hut, and they all smiled at him.

"Thank you, dear Herr Grieg," they said. "We have never heard more beautiful music."

One young girl, looking rosy and pretty in her Norwegian

national dress, came up to him. She smiled as she spoke and looked around at the green forest. "Everything here seems to sing *Solveig's Song*," she said. "Will you play it for us?"

Grieg could not refuse, and the delicate song floating out of the "tune house" truly seemed to be an expression of the spirit of the forest. But after he had finished, Grieg had to explain that he was composing, and that quiet was necessary for him.

The people nodded. "Of course," they said. "But we will make no sound. We will do nothing to disturb."

"It isn't only quiet," Grieg answered. "I must have privacy. I have to feel that I am alone to get the music to come right."

At last, they went off, but Grieg could not get to work again. In the days that followed, although Grieg's wishes were known, the "tune house" proved impossible for the people to resist. It was not far from a road, and the people, hearing the sounds of music, could not believe that Grieg would be disturbed by a few moments of listening. Grieg would hear the stealthy footsteps and the sound of someone settling himself carefully in the grass.

Something had to be done, and Grieg decided that he would be "like a new Aladdin" and remove his castle. He found a place, far from the footpath, down by the fjord. When Grieg announced his plans, the country people offered to help, and Grieg's Aladdin-like move became a regular American house-moving "bee."

A feast was arranged to take place at the end of the moving. Grieg laid in a supply of cakes and sweet biscuits and a barrel of Hardanger ale. The small army of men with Grieg at their head then advanced on the little hut, and, with a mighty tug, it was pulled from its foundation. The women and children who were present waved their handkerchiefs and shouted hurrahs. Off went the little house, sometimes dragged and sometimes rolled on the trunks of trees to its new home. The new site in the birch grove close to the clear waters of the fjord was even more inviting than the place on the hillside. When it was put in place, the men ran back for the piano. Grieg laughed heartily when he saw how they brought it. They came galloping up with it as though it were merely a feather. Then it was time for the food. After the feast, Grieg played for all the people.

Some of them crowded into the hut around the piano so that there was scarcely room for Grieg to raise his arms. Others stood outside, or leaned on the window to see the playing. Grieg played a folk dance, and another, and another, until everyone was dancing and clapping and feeling the merriment of the dedication of the little house. At last, when Grieg was tired and simply could not play any more, one of the crowd stood up and gave a toast.

"Good luck to the house!" he shouted. The others joined him in the wish. "Good luck to the house!" Then there was one more toast which was also called out heartily. "Skaal to all the people of the South Fjord!"

Grieg, looking round and seeing all the hearty good will, played once again. He began gaily, but as he played, the mood of his music changed, turned melancholy and dream-like, and the people sat down in the grass to listen. At first they threw pine cones at each other and laughed with the music, but soon, as in the case of Grieg, the lyrical beauty of the fjord and the dignity of the mountains established an atmosphere of respect. Each person sat silently, and Grieg's

187

music, turning from major to minor, expressed the dream thoughts and feelings of the people. It was in this quiet mood that the dedication of the "tune house" ended.

During the summer and winter, Grieg worked in the little hut. Sometimes the storms came up, and the little house shook with the furious winds and threatened to fly with Grieg up into the sky. Other times, the fjord was like glass, clear and silent, and the shadows of the mountains and trees were so distinct that one could imagine they were real.

Near the end of Grieg's stay on the Hardanger, on the occasion of his birthday, the great Ole Bull came to help with the celebration. The day was perfect, bright and blue, and the music of the waterfalls carried clearly in the quiet air. Ole Bull came with his party and brought with him his famous violin. At once he took charge and played the famous violin so merrily that the day became a festival of music. At the end, he called the peasants together and made one of his hearty speeches. He spoke first of the beauty of the fjord, the shining water, the blooming apple trees, and the ranges of lofty mountain peaks. And then, beaming at the crowd, he concluded by telling them that their tiny village of Lofthus had won immortality because Edvard Grieg, Norway's great composer, had lived there and was writing great music there.

CHAPTER 9

SUCCESS AT LAST

The little blond gentleman who frequently sailed from Norway to conduct the famous orchestras of Europe had become very famous. He conducted in all the centers of music, in Vienna, Leipsig, Rotterdam, Amsterdam, Rome, Paris, and London. Everywhere he was welcomed with great acclaim.

Once in Leipsig, he met Franz Liszt again. He played his piano concerto which was now so famous, and although this time Liszt did not rise up and go striding off singing out powerfully the melody, Grieg knew that he approved because he heard, from the box on his left where his friend sat, Liszt's well-known grunt of approval.

In Amsterdam, Grieg was so popular that in the shops the people said, "It is surely Herr Grieg whom I have the pleasure of addressing." And on the streets, a stranger who wanted to speak to the famous creator of *Peer Gynt* would come up and say, "Perhaps Herr Grieg would like to know the way." And when Grieg would shake his head and say that he knew Amsterdam well, the stranger might invite him into one of the Dutch restaurants for a feast of Dutch oysters. Grieg liked to tell these stories later. "I can tell

189

you it's a life here!" he wrote to his publisher. "Ten sheets I could write on it. On the Dutch oysters twice as many."

In London, Grieg conquered completely; and in Paris, when Nina appeared with him in a concert, both he and Nina took the hearts of the Parisians by storm. When Nina came on the concert stage to sing her husband's songs, the audience was at first startled. They were accustomed to seeing prima donnas self-assured, strikingly dressed, and decorated with handsome jewels. Madame Grieg was like no concert singer they had ever seen. She was as simple in manner as Grieg, and odd in the same interesting way. She wore no make-up at all, a high-necked brown silk dress, and her hair was cut short and brushed up. She curtsied to the audience, just as she curtsied to the Queen of Sweden when she sang for her. She then turned to her husband, began to sing, and went directly to everyone's heart. She thought only of her song, not at all of herself or the audience, and the result was entirely different from the usual effect created by a prima donna. The applause for Nina Grieg as for Edvard Grieg was tremendous. And, just as though she were a young girl, she gave her court curtsy after every round of thundering applause.

When the critics wrote the next day of the concert, there were words of praise for both Edvard and Nina Grieg. Of Grieg, one wrote, "Grieg is the living, thrilling incarnation of Norway."

Another wrote, "His fresh inspiration and the melancholy poetry of his words have conquered the old hearts one by one."

Of Nina, one critic wrote: "As a singer of Norse songs that he has set to music, she is matchless. . . . The delicacy,

Grieg's music was the incarnation of Norway.

the purity, the pathos that she infused into her song were beyond all praise. She was given up to the song, and did not trouble herself about Nina Grieg, or how she looked, or what people thought of her."

Of all those who wrote of Grieg's music, the one who best described it was not a critic at all, but himself a composer and very great musician. He was the great Russian, Tschaikovsky, who wrote of Grieg's music: "What charm, what inimitable and rich musical imagery! What warmth and passion in his melodic phrases, what teeming vitality in his harmony, what originality and beauty in the turn of his piquant and ingenious modulations and rhythms, and in all the rest what interest, novelty, and independence!"

So the concerts went for Grieg now, successfully and crowned with praise. During the earlier years, Grieg was accustomed to read unfavorable criticism. He felt some of it keenly, and once wrote in an essay some words which told how he felt. He referred to a certain man "as a typical critic who lies down like a wet dog on just the best places." The critics were no longer like wet dogs for Grieg. That time was all in the past.

Grieg never came to the United States although he was many times invited to come. When one of his American friends asked him why he would not come, Grieg's blue eyes twinkled. "I cannot put up with seasickness," he said, "but I would come if you can guarantee that the Atlantic will behave itself." Then he looked at his friend again and quickly added, "But, mind you, it must be a written guarantee."

The years passed, and Grieg continued to live the same kind of life. He traveled during some of the winters and enjoyed seeing the countries of Europe, hearing music, and meeting the interesting people of the world. But always, when he was away, he longed for the mountains of Norway. In one letter written from a southern land, he said, "No, the home of wildness, of mystery, I know very well where that is to be found."

In the middle years of his life, he built his home on a hill with such stately views of mountain and fjord that he lived always in the land of *Peer Gynt*. He called his house by the interesting name of *Troldhaugen*, which means the hill of the trolls. Here in his home of mystery, home of wildness, he lived and worked. He had built near *Troldhaugen* a little work hut such as he always needed to have. In summer the trees and wild flowers were all around it, and in winter, there were the gleaming mountains and the piled-up snow. It is not strange that his best songs continued to be those based upon Norwegian themes, the folk songs and the forest moods.

He worked through most of the days and did not welcome visitors until after four o'clock. At the entrance gate to *Troldhaugen*, there was a sign: *Edvard Grieg onsker at vare uforstyrrd til klokken 4 eftermiddag.* This said: *Edvard Grieg does not wish to receive callers until after 4.* Only after that hour was there sociability at the Hill of the Trolls.

Rikard Nordraak, the friend of his youth, was often in his thoughts. And Nordraak's words of confidence continued to inspire him to write his music of the Northland. One composition which was close to Grieg's heart is now very famous. It is called *Ballade in G Minor*. The music is strong and in a minor key. The words could almost be taken as a motto for Grieg's work.

"Many a bonny song I know
Of lands under warmer skies;
But never yet have I heard the song
Of what at our doorstep lies.

"So now I'll try if I cannot make
A song that will let folk see
How fine it is in the North country
The South treats so scornfully."

Grieg wrote music to the end of his life, and continued to live on the Hill of the Trolls among the beautiful Norwegian scenes. Today, if you visit Norway, you can see a statue of him in the town gardens at Bergen. It stands surrounded by green growing things, and is not so very far from another statue, one of Ole Bull. The one man, the tall and handsome Ole Bull, gave Norway an ambassador to carry her name out over the world. The other, Edvard Grieg, little, delicate, sensitive, more highly gifted for creation, was able to give the greater gift, a lasting music that can always speak for Norway and tell of her scenes, her people, and the strange, and wild fairytale beauty of the land of *Peer Gynt*.

THE STORY OF FRIDTJOF NANSEN

FRIDTJOF NANSEN

1861-1930

Fridtjof Nansen was like a Norwegian viking, bold, strong, and handsome. He was a great Arctic explorer and a distinguished scientist. His book, Farthest North, *is one of the great adventure books of all time. In the late years of his life, after World War I, he worked for war sufferers, for war refugees, and for a League of Nations in which all the countries would work together for the good of the world. In his day, Norway was no longer the small, isolated, fairy-tale corner of the world that Ole Bull, and Grieg, and Ibsen talked about. It was now a modern nation, fully participating in the life of the world. In this new national life, Fridtjof Nansen was Norway's strongest leader.*

CHAPTER I

BOY ON SKIS

A few miles out of the city of Oslo, during the days of the American Civil War, there was a large old family estate called *Store Froen*. It was the home of Fru Adelaide Nansen and Herr Baldur Nansen. They had a large family of boys who filled all the rooms of the house with noisy activity.

Of these boys, the most interesting one was Fridtjof. He was blue-eyed, fair-haired, sturdy, and active. As a tiny boy, he learned to swim and splash in the river that ran through the garden, and when he was only four had already learned to enjoy the winter snow and to manage well his first pair of skis. These first skis did not please him. They had been cut down from a pair that had belonged to an older brother, and one had turned out to be longer than the other. In addition to this matter of the unequal length, there was nothing likable about these skis, nothing to catch the fancy.

One day near the end of the winter, Fridtjof went off to the forest with his brothers. He simply could not keep up. The snow was wet and thin, and the made-over skis behaved particularly badly. Finally when he was almost home, the little boy kicked them off in disgust and sat down at the side of the road.

"How can I keep up with skis like these?" he thought.

The more Fridtjof thought about what skis should be like, the worse his present pair appeared to be. He frowned and felt as though he would not be able to keep from crying if he couldn't have better skis than this awful, cut-down, unequal pair. As he sat in the snow, the town printer, Herr Fabritius, came by. Herr Fabritius was surprised to see the little boy sitting forlornly, and looking both sad and worn out.

"Hello, Fridtjof Nansen," he said. "What are you doing sitting in the snow? Why aren't you going on with your brothers?"

"I must have some new skis," said Fridtjof soberly. "These are not good."

"And what is wrong with them?"

"They are not good. One is longer than the other." Fridtjof stood the skis up in the snow.

Herr Fabritius looked at them carefully. "I see they are not right," he said at last. "How old are you, Fridtjof?"

"Four."

"Indeed." Herr Fabritius paused thoughtfully. "Yes, I see that you are old enough for better skis. I see that clearly. Well, do you know what I will do for you? I am going to get you a fine new pair. But you must not be in a hurry. Spring will soon be here, and soon after that, the summer. When winter comes again, the skis will be here. The time will not really be long, but it will appear so to you. Can you wait patiently?"

Fridtjof had jumped up. He did not take his eyes from Herr Fabritius' face. "Oh yes, sir," he said. And then, because he could not wait to tell his mother and his brothers, he ran off in a hurry, and left Herr Fabritius standing alone in the road.

Herr Fabritius shrugged his shoulders and laughed heartily. "What a fine sturdy Norwegian that boy is! He will make good use of the skis. One can be sure of that."

Within a few weeks after this day that was so important in the life of young Fridtjof, the snow was gone from the roads. Slowly it vanished from the garden at *Store Froen*, from the shaded places, and finally from the depths of the near-by forest of Nordmarka. Spring was in the air, the wonderful spring of Norway. The lakes were free and clear of ice and reflected the blue sky. The cascades and waterfalls of Nordmarka forest came alive and went splashing their way into the lakes and streams. Soon the first leaves and the first flowers were out. The Nansen boys fished in the streams, collected leaves and berries, and carried on wars with the neighborhood boys and with the forest squirrels.

But while all the games and forest adventures went on and on through the long bright summer days, Fridtjof always remembered the promise of Herr Fabritius. When the summer ended at last, and when one morning, there was the first trace of hoar frost on the ground, the promise came back to him so clearly that he ran from the house out to the road and stood where he knew Herr Fabritius would come riding by. He waited for a long time. The day of the promise seemed long ago now. What if Herr Fabritius had forgotten all about it? Fridtjof sat down on a rock and pulled his cap over his ears. He could not keep his thoughts from the promised skis. At last, far down the road, he saw Herr Fabritius coming. He jumped up and planted himself in the middle of the road.

When Herr Fabritius came up to Fridtjof, he pulled up his horse. "Good morning," he said. "You are out early."

"There is some snow," the little boy answered. "Winter is here. What about the skis?"

Herr Fabritius laughed. "So that is your business with me! Yes, you shall have them right enough. Only be patient. The snow for skiing is not here yet."

On the next morning, Fridtjof was again in the road. "What about the skis today?" he asked.

Each morning for several weeks, Fridtjof stood in the road and asked the same question, and each morning, Herr Fabritius gave the same answer. The two of them examined together the hoar frost, and although Herr Fabritius was doubtful concerning its thickness and slipperiness, Fridtjof was certain that the skis would slide along well.

Then one night the first real snow of winter came. It was a wonderfully soft luxuriant snow that changed the world into gleaming slides and jumps and beautiful trackless spaces. Fridtjof was just getting up when his sister called him in great excitement. "Fridtjof, Fridtjof, come quickly. Here is a tremendously long package for you."

Fridtjof came running. When he pulled away the wrapping, he found a magnificent pair of skis made of ash, red-lacquered, and with trim black stripes. There was also a long blue-lacquered shaft with a knob that would fit in his hand. He turned them 'round and 'round so that he could examine all the parts. He had never seen such beautiful skis, such marvels of length, so hard, so gleaming. Here were skis to take one's fancy! Here were skis to lose one's heart to. As soon as he was dressed, he put the skis on and was off. At first they seemed long and difficult, but in only a few minutes he could manage them. They ran smoothly. The blue knob was right for his hand, and the staff comfortable and secure. All of the morning, Fridtjof walked with his skis on the new snow, and never before had the snow world appeared to him so beautiful and mysterious.

By the end of the morning, Fridtjof and his skis were old friends. He had tried most of the short slopes. There was, however, one hill called Huseby Hill which was forbidden to the Nansen boys. It was the place of the older ski jumpers and was both long and steep. This Huseby Hill began to get into Fridtjof's mind. Finally he went to it, and, like most of the smaller boys, tried it from the middle of the slope. All went well. He kept his feet and leveled out easily at the bottom. Soon he tried again, this time from a higher point, and again all went well. After that, he stood watching one of the other boys start from the top. Though this boy was much older than he, nothing would now do but that he also must start from the top.

From there, the slope appeared long and slippery. Could he really make it? Yet surely the wonderful new skis could take him safely. Off he went. In a moment he was going like the wind, and a moment later was approaching the jump at frantic speed. He tried to think how to manage this jump, but all at once before he had time for thinking, he was sailing through the air. How had he come so high and at such a terrifying speed? All at once the ski flew ahead of him, and he, after making a high arc in the air, plunged head first into a snowdrift.

For a long moment, there was silence on Huseby Hill. The bigger boys looked at each other and their eyes were frightened. Why hadn't they stopped so little a boy from making the jump? Fridtjof must have broken his neck. But as they watched, Fridtjof's legs began to kick, and in a moment more he was scrambling out. The sight was so funny, the waving legs so energetic, and the relief so great, that a shout went up. All the skiers on the hill from the top to the bottom doubled over with laughter. Two of the boys pulled Fridtjof to his feet.

"Are you all right?" they said.

The little boy blinked, rubbed the snow from his face, and tried to get his breath. "Where are my skis?" he asked anxiously.

The boys ran to see. They pulled the skis from a snow drift. The skis had driven in with such force that the boys had to tug to get them out. However, they appeared sound and whole. "They're all right, Fridtjof," they shouted. "Come and see for yourself."

Fridtjof felt each ski carefully and could find no break or scratch. Only then did he turn to the boys and laugh.

"You flew through the air like a hawk," said one.

"It's lucky you aimed for a big drift," said another.

"Yes," Fridtjof nodded. He picked up the skis and, this time holding them carefully, went home. The day had turned out well. The beautiful skis were not scratched. Still he was glad to go home and to wait for another day before trying them again.

During the next months and years, Fridtjof Nansen would become the complete master of the beautiful ski. He would conquer Huseby Hill and later the more difficult wilderness slopes of the Norwegian mountains. He would grow strong and so skillful that none could compete with him. In addition to physical skill, he had, in remarkable degree for a young boy, another quality. This was a deep love for nature, particularly the great and somber Norwegian scenes. He loved the stately pine forests, the mountains and crags both in sunlight and moonlight, and the long snow hills with their pure white unbroken lines. Often when he was out, he stood doing nothing and staring.

"Do stop dawdling," his brothers said.

Fridtjof was not able to explain why it was that he wanted to stand and look and look until he could get the wonderfully beautiful scenes inside of his mind.

The forest of Nordmarka, which began only a few miles away from the Nansen farm, was beautiful and extensive, a vast wonderland of almost unbroken wildness.

By the time Fridtjof was twelve years old, he knew many parts of Nordmarka well. He was old enough so that his parents allowed him to go there alone, and he and his brother, Alexander, often went to spend several days at a time. They liked to live like Robinson Crusoe, and were proud when they could go with nothing more than some matches and a loaf of bread in their pockets. They would set out at noon on Saturday, go directly to the forest, and then for several hours would tramp into it to find a favorite place by the river. Once there, out came the fishing rods, and the two boys would cast away as long as the daylight lasted. As the string of trout grew long, the boys' enthusiasm grew so that neither could bear to stop until the real dark came. Then how wonderful it was to light a fire, to broil the fresh fish in the embers, to sit eating and loafing. The black forest, the fragrant slight night breezes, and the sounds of the forest creatures settling drowsily—all of these were pleasant and familiar to them. Then they would creep under a bush and sleep soundly until the dawn woke them and set them to fishing again.

Often the boys spent two or three days in this way in the forest. Once they spent thirteen full days and nights and lived all of the time, with the exception of bread and coffee, on food that they found in the forest.

So the childhood years passed for Fridtjof Nansen.

When he was eighteen, he was six feet tall, and broad-shouldered. He was handsome and striking to see, fair-haired, blue-eyed, sturdy, like a Norwegian viking.

"That's Fridtjof Nansen," people would say, speaking always with admiration. And well they might, for the tall young viking was ready to begin a highly adventurous and noble career.

CHAPTER 2

LUCKY STAR

One winter afternoon in an office at the University of Oslo, Fridtjof Nansen sat talking with one of his instructors, Professor Collett.

"It is always difficult," the Professor was saying, "to find the work one is best suited for. You are interested in science. You are also an athlete, an expert sportsman, and a good shot. It is this combination of interests that makes me think you may welcome a suggestion that I have to make. Perhaps you have heard me talk of a friend who is the captain of a sealing vessel, *The Viking*. He is soon to sail northward for the season's seal hunt. The life is strenuous, but full of adventure. Why not go along? Enjoy yourself, see another part of the world, make observations, keep records, and get some training in scientific research. I am certain I can arrange the trip for you. It will give you a chance to try out a life of observation."

Nansen was immediately enthusiastic. "Can you really arrange it? I can imagine nothing better. What a chance to see the Arctic!"

"Most young Norwegians want to see the North," said Professor Collett. "I think it must be that so much of it is still romantic and unexplored. It is a land of mystery. Well, come back in a week. I will give you my report. I am sure it will be favorable."

When Fridtjof came back a week later, the answer was yes. The captain of the sealer would be glad to have a sturdy and capable young man to help with the sealing.

Fridtjof was elated. The adventurous life, the chance to see the northern mists, the world of ice floes and towering icebergs, herds of seal and polar bears, perhaps Iceland and Greenland—all of this was incredible luck.

Norway looked beautiful to him as the boat sailed off. The pine woods were fragrant, and hundreds of birds flew over the rocks and the myriad islets. He stood watching as long as he could see the land, then went to his cabin, arranged his things neatly, and then went up and began to acquaint himself with the men on the sealer.

For seven days and nights the ship sailed northward. Stiff gales came and swept over the decks, and in the evening, there was phosphorescence like colored flames in the water.

Suddenly on the evening of the seventh day, after the dark had already come, Nansen had his first sight of the mysterious arctic world that had been in his thoughts for so many days. The ship was plunging steadily forward. He had gone below and was working at his table when he heard the men shout.

"Ice—ice ahead! Ice ahead!"

Nansen rushed on deck. At first he saw nothing that was different, but then, as he looked out intently into the blackness, he saw something huge and white. As the ship came closer, he saw that it was a white islet of ice. Then there was another, and another, and then many more, till the sea was filled with ice floes. They were like bobbing white ghosts appearing and fading away again in the dark. Far to the north, on the horizon's edge, there was a curious and glowing brightness, a mysterious half-light. Coming from the same direction, there was a dull roaring which was like the sound of surf beating on rocks.

As Nansen wondered what the light and the roaring could be, the captain of the sealer came and stood by his side. "It's a great sight, isn't it?" he said. "I envy you seeing it for the first time. Do you know what it is? The light which you see in the sky is made by the drift ice. It throws its reflection on the sky. The noise is the sea breaking on the ice floes. Sometimes the noise of the floes crashing against each other is like terrible thunder."

To the captain, the sight was old and familiar, but to Fridtjof Nansen, it was a world completely new, awesome, and enthralling. The scene absorbed him so completely that he was startled when the captain turned the talk to business.

"Tomorrow I hope to come on the seals," said the captain. "The sealing must begin in a day or two if we are to get a full cargo."

The captain went below, but Fridtjof continued to stare at the dark northern horizon. The ship plunged on with greater difficulty through the heavy seas. The floes were larger, giant ghosts in the dark, and the horizon continued to be pale and faintly glowing.

The next day there was storm. The ship quivered and groaned and made her way slowly through the ice. To the captain's distress, there was no sign of the seals. After the days of storm came several days of fog, and the ship sailed through mists like wool.

The ship drifted with the ice.

"When will the weather clear?" the men asked. "When will we find the seals?"

"We must find the seals," said the worried captain. "It is a matter of thousands of dollars for the investors and hundreds for the seal hunters."

The next day everyone kept looking for the seals on the ice, but they had no luck. The day after that there was a hurricane, and then fog, and days of searching which stretched out to five weeks.

"Where are the seals? Where are the seals?" the captain kept asking. "We have lost the prize for this year."

In the middle of June, the ship had a bout with the ice.

Great ice blocks knocked into her and set up such a groaning and trembling that all on board feared for their safety. By a miracle they came through, and in the morning, there was once more a clear sky and open water. The captain was cheerful as he talked to the steward.

"I am certain that we shall get some seals today," he said. "Don't you remember, steward, how last time the ice played us these tricks, we sailed straight into the seals and took over nine hundred?"

And the captain was right. Hurrah for the seals! By evening there were hundreds, lying on flat ice. The boats were lowered. The gun shots cracked. The battle lasted three days. No one slept, and a good haul was made.

But luck turned again. Within a few days, the ship froze in the ice off the coast of Greenland, and for the entire month was a prisoner of the ice. This last ill fortune was a great blow to the men and to the captain. A month of inactivity at the height of the sealing season coming after the weeks of disappointment meant that they could not hope for much from the expedition.

The ship drifted with the ice. All around was the white snow-and-ice world, the home of the white polar bear. Nansen went hunting with the others, and one day when he was out with the captain and one of the sailors, he saw a huge bear shambling off. In his excitement at seeing the great creature, Nansen rushed after him. When he came to a broad pool of water, he was in such a hurry that he forgot to be cautious. He rushed at it, making a good spring to carry him across. As he landed, the ice gave way and he plunged into the icy water. His first thought was for his rifle. He pitched it up on the ice, but it slipped down again into the water. Nansen dived for it and got it, and this time threw it up on the ice and scrambled after it. In the meantime, the bear had gone considerable distance, and now, as Nansen looked, he was just disappearing behind an ice hummock. Off Nansen raced. When he came to the knoll, he peered over it and was face to face with the bear. He lifted his rifle, but before he shot, the bear had turned around and plunged into another pool which had been hidden by the ice hummock.

And now began a race. Nansen sprang over the hummock and rushed to the edge of the ice. Where was the bear? As Nansen watched, he saw something move at the bottom of the ice pool. It was the white bear swimming easily to the other side. Nansen saw a small floe near the bear, and without thinking, he leaped across the water on to this floe. It rocked under him, but held his weight, and in another minute, up came the head of the bear near the floe. He began to roar, and then clambered up on the floe and came toward Nansen. By this time Nansen had recovered his balance, and he sent a bullet into the bear. In a few moments more, the captain and the sailor came up and they helped to skin the huge creature and to carry back the heavy skin to the ship. This bear was one of the biggest that Nansen ever got. He was always proud of this battle with his enemy. When he went home, he had the luxuriant skin made into a fur rug for his study, and he liked to say as he sat comfortably at his writing table, "Here I sit with my foot on my enemy's neck."

On other days, there were other battles. By the end of the month, Nansen had shot thirteen white polar bears. The men liked to talk of these battles. "My word!" said one of them. "That Nansen, he's a great fellow for bears."

Sometimes the men built fires on the ice and burned the blubber and roasted the steaks. No food had ever tasted so good.

While Nansen lived this life of adventure, he also lived the life of the ship's scientist. He kept accurate records of the temperatures and the ice drift. He threw dip nets into the water and took dredgings which he studied under his microscope. He noted the kinds of birds and their habits. He studied the habits of the seal, and one day found a young seal which he took aboard and fed and tended carefully for eight days. He tried to take pictures of this baby seal and posed it carefully on the hatch of the boat. But before he could get his camera out, it always began to flap about, and the picture was nothing but a blur.

All the while, during all the month that the ship was frozen in, over on the horizon lay the Greenland coast, glittering and tempting like something in a dream. Through many nights, Nansen watched and studied the distant island. One day he asked the captain for permission to make his way ashore, going over the ice and taking a boat for the open spaces. The captain refused, saying that the trip was too dangerous.

"Someday," Nansen thought, "I shall return and see what Greenland is like."

Some years later, after Fridtjof Nansen had become one of the great explorers of the Arctic, including this vast island of Greenland, he liked to say that everything happened as it did to him because of his "lucky star." He wrote in a letter:

"Is it not really wonderful? If any one may be excused for believing in his lucky star, it is surely I—so often have extraordinary chances happened, just at the crucial moments of my life, which seemed to point the way for me."

Nansen liked to think that his lucky star caused him to be set down off the glittering coast of Greenland, and that it kept him drifting there for twenty-four days and nights. He liked to think that it was because of this time on the ice that he was drawn irresistibly to explore Greenland, and after Greenland, the mysterious regions round the North Pole.

CHAPTER 3

GREENLAND CALLS

Back in Norway, Nansen settled to work in a museum in
Bergen. He had a fine microscope, and with it, he began the
study of the development of small animal life. He found
this world under the microscope just as curious and wonderful
as the vast Arctic. How complex life appeared to be! How
curious and puzzling and logical! He decided to take a doctor's degree in science at the university. After the long hours
of studious work in the museum and the university, he often
escaped to walk in the mountains, or descend the steep slopes
on his skis. He particularly enjoyed skiing by moonlight
when the world was vast and silent and full of stars. On
these nights, he liked to think of Greenland and the old
dream of exploring it.

"Someday I will go," he told himself. "It is time someone
explores the mysterious Ice Cap."

By the winter of 1887, he was ready to begin working out
his plans. He burst in one evening upon a friend of his, Dr.
Grieg of Bergen. He was excited and flung himself down on
a sofa to talk. "Do you know what I'm going to set about
now?" he asked. "I mean to have a try at crossing Greenland."

"What! What did you say?" said his astonished friend.

Nansen calmly pulled out an atlas and pointed out the way he had decided to go. "I shall just wait to take my doctor's degree in the spring and then be off."

Dr. Grieg listened to the bold and confident words, and at the same time he saw in his mind the vast cold stretches of unknown Greenland. "It sounds like magnificent madness to me," he said.

The remarkable thing about all these plans was that Nansen made them all work out. He took his doctor's degree in the spring. He went to Stockholm and talked with the great explorer, Nordenskjold, who had made a ski run on Greenland of about eighty miles. Nordenskjold was greatly impressed with Nansen and offered at once to place his experience at the young man's service. The expedition fired the imagination of a wealthy merchant from Denmark who offered to finance it. Nansen made ready all the physical equipment, giving everything his careful attention. He designed his own sledges, made them of wood, sturdy and light. They could be lashed together and fitted with sails so that they could run like ice boats. Nansen also studied the language of the Eskimo so that he could talk with them when he came to the west coast settlements where they lived.

When most people heard of the Nansen expedition, they scoffed. "Fridtjof Nansen's a fool and a dreamer," they said. "He can never cross Greenland. The party will die on the Ice Cap. Why doesn't he stick to his laboratory?"

They did not stop to think that Norwegians had always been explorers. In the long ago times, bold viking ships had pushed farther and farther west and north. They had discovered new lands and seas. On the empty spaces of the world's map, they had drawn in the outlines and crossed out the words, *Unknown* and *Unexplored*.

The story of Nansen's expedition to Greenland is full of adventures. He took five Norwegians with him and two Lapps called Balto and Ravna. These Lapps wore four-cornered caps, trousers of reindeer skin, and long tunics to the knees. Ravna had lived all of his life in a tent in Finn-marken, and he owned a herd of three hundred reindeer.

For weeks, the men toiled through the snow, over difficult crevasses and snow bridges. The temperatures were 40° and 50° of frost. To Nansen, at least, in spite of all the difficulties, the scenes were beautiful. The snow was a huge white carpet glittering with diamonds. Sometimes when the snow storms came, there was nothing to do but pitch the tents, crawl in the sleeping bags, draw up the covers well, eat biscuit and dried meat and try to sleep. At such times Ravna was gloomy.

"I am an old Lapp," he said. "I know what a snowstorm is upon the mountains in September. You won't see the end of it yet awhile."

When the sun shone, the men wore snow spectacles and red silk veils. These red silk veils fluttering against the blue sky, and worn by the grimy men, made an odd sight.

In the mornings, things were usually cheerful. The cooking machine produced hot chocolate or coffee. The men took it in bed and enjoyed the snugness of their tiny tent house. Ravna was in charge of water for the coffee and cooking. As an old Lapp who always had had to use snow to get water for cooking, he knew what was the best kind for melting. He dug down deeply to get the old coarse snow which melted into far more water than the new light fall.

214

By the middle of September, when the men had been five weeks in the snow, and it seemed as if this strange life had gone on forever, Nansen found that the land was declining. It was clear they were coming to the west coast. There were other cheerful signs. A snow bunting came flying toward them. The little bird, the first live creature they had seen, was like a messenger welcoming them back to the world of living things.

"Our blessings on you," called Nansen to the bird.

On September 19 a wind came up, and Nansen ordered sails to be hoisted on the sledges. Off they went at a speed to take the breath away, and by the middle of the afternoon, after the day of flying, Balto shouted, "Land ahead!"

There it was, through the snow mists, far away, yet clearly to be seen, the wonderful and longed-for sight, a long dark bare ridge. They continued to sail by moonlight, the sledges looking like viking ships with their square sails. In the morning, on the horizon ahead, the land lay bare of snow. The men were like children as they gazed.

Imagine the surprise of the West Coast Eskimos when they saw the explorers appear. They welcomed Nansen with a great shout and gave him the Eskimo name *Angisorsuak* which means *The Very Big One.*

The Very Big One laughed heartily at this title. The Eskimos were particularly interested in the Lapps. Old Ravna liked to sit cross-legged in the Eskimo huts for hours at a time, saying nothing at all, but enjoying all the admiration. He said to Nansen, "I, old Lapp, don't like all these people about, but I show how we Lapps drive reindeer."

It was found that the last ship for Europe had gone and that Nansen's party would have to spend the winter with the

Eskimos. This was a great disappointment at first, but the winter proved to be unusually interesting. The men made Eskimo friends and learned to know about Eskimo life. *The Very Big One* learned to eat Eskimo food, raw blubber and raw halibut skin. He learned to manage the Eskimo boats, the kayaks, to stalk reindeer, and to fish for halibut and whale. To his astonishment, there were some Eskimos so bold as to leap on a wounded whale and ride him to give the death blow.

The Greenland Eskimos became so fond of *The Very Big One* that when he stayed out too long in the kayak at the fishing they always became worried. When at last Nansen would show up, the whole group stood on the shore and shouted, *"Kujunak, Kujunak, Nansen tigipok, a jungilak,"* which means "Let us give thanks, Nansen has come, all is well."

After the hard but interesting winter, the ship from Europe came in the spring and took Nansen and his party home. They had been gone a little over a year. Hundreds of sailboats came out to meet them and cheer them when they came up the Oslo Fjord. Nansen was no longer an unknown and crazy dreamer. He had carried through the difficult expedition. He was the first to cross Greenland and tell the world of what the land of ice was like. He had collected data on temperatures and winds and currents and made known another portion of the great world.

As the ship came up the Oslo Fjord, one of the men looked from the cheering crowds to Ravna. "Are not all these people a fine sight, Ravna?" he asked.

"Yes," answered the little Lapp. "Yes, very fine; if they had only been reindeer."

CHAPTER 4

THE VOYAGE TO THE POLE

Five years passed before Nansen took up the life of an explorer again. During this time, he worked at the University of Oslo, became a professor, and did outstanding work. He married Eva Sars, a beautiful and talented woman who later become a concert singer. They built a house and called it *Godthaab* which means *Good Hope*, after the town in Greenland. They had a baby daughter, Liv, who was a great delight to her young father. Nansen wrote books, a wonderful story called *First Crossing of Greenland*, and another, *Life Among the Eskimo*.

While he did all of these things, he continued to dream of exploring the Arctic—all those mysterious wastes at the top of the world which had never been seen by man. As the trip on the sealing vessel had led him to explore Greenland, so the trip across Greenland made him want to go farther north, to the North Pole itself. Sometimes when a friend asked him why he wanted to go off exploring, Nansen did not understand him.

"Man wants to know," he said. "When he ceases to do so, he is no longer man."

Then it happened that in June 1881, there was a curious and dramatic discovery. Up north of Siberia, near the New Siberian Islands, three years before this time, a ship called the *Jeanette* had been sunk. The dramatic discovery was that some articles from this ship were found in the drift ice off the southwest coast of Greenland. When Nansen read the report, he was immediately excited.

"That is the way I shall explore the Arctic," he thought. "Go in a strongly built vessel to the North Siberian Islands. Allow the boat to freeze in the ice. The polar currents will then carry it west, past the Pole, and finally out into the sea near Greenland. The expedition would take possibly three years. It would matter little if the exact mathematical point which is the Pole is reached. The important thing is to investigate the unknown regions around the Pole."

The more Nansen thought about this new plan, the more certain he became that it would work out. He talked to a ship-builder, Colin Archer by name. Together they planned a ship that could get through the polar ice. It would have to be enormously strong. The bottom would be rounded so that the ice could not grip the sides and squeeze them together. Instead the ice would push up the rounded bottom so that the ship could ride securely.

Time passed, the careful plans were made. Ship and supplies were ready, and all foreseeable emergencies planned for. The ship would carry provisions for twelve men for five years. She had eight boats and warm tents to be used if the men had to leave the ship and make their way home across the ice floes. The crew was carefully chosen. The captain was Sverdrup who had gone with Nansen on the Greenland expedition. Nansen's wife christened the ship.

At a special ceremony before thousands of people, she broke a bottle of champagne against the stem of the vessel and said in a loud clear voice, "I name you *Fram*."

The word *Fram* means *Forward*. The ship would prove to be rightly named. Boldly, steadily, resolutely she would go on the most adventurous of all trips of exploration, the dangerous trip to the North Pole.

At last, on Midsummer Day, 1893, the *Fram* was ready to sail. There she lay, puffing and waiting the signal. People crowded the docks all waving hats and handkerchiefs.

Nansen was late in coming, and when he came, he pushed through the crowds and went quickly on board and gave the signal to start. The people were surprised at his expression. His face was calm, fixed, hard, as though he were holding down his emotion. It was the great day for him, the start of the great long-dreamed-of adventure, but it was also a terribly difficult day. He had just said good-by to his wife and child, and to the home that meant so much to him. For a few moments he wondered why he was going.

"Behind me lay all I hold dear in life," he thought. "And what before me? How many years will pass ere I shall see it all again?"

Slowly, quietly the *Fram* turned out to sea. The people cheered, and all the little pleasure boats sent up a burst of tooting and blowing. Nansen stood on the bridge. He waved at the people, then turned his glass toward his home. He could see it clearly, brought close by the powerful lens, a stretch of meadow, pine ridges behind, the loved house, and the summer-clad figure of his wife by the bench under the fir tree. With the aid of the glass, he said his second and final farewell.

Out into the fjord! Into rainy weather that suited Nansen's melancholy mood. Quickly the bay and the loved coast faded out. The *Fram* was off. The strong bonds with home were broken.

The second day and those immediately following it were brilliant, golden, blue, and clear. It was as though Norway wished to appear fair to her departing sons, to store up in their minds against the cold bleak days to come the scenes of striking beauty. Nansen stood on deck and could not have enough of looking at his land. The ship passed Bergen with its mountains, sparkling and glittering. Here many little boats gaily decked with bunting came out of the harbor to escort the *Fram*. They passed Trondheim, the ancient capital. Torghatten and Hestemanden, Lovirnen, and Traen. Lofoten, and all the lovely places, wild and beautiful in the mountains.

One day as Nansen stood looking, he saw an old woman standing alone on a high bare crag. She was waving and waving.

"I wonder if it can really be us she is waving to," said Nansen to the pilot.

"You may be sure it is," the pilot answered.

"But how can she know who we are?"

"Oh! they know all about the *Fram* up here, in every cabin, and they will be on the lookout for you as you come back, I can tell you."

On other days, fishing boats came out to the *Fram* and the fishermen gazed in admiration at her. They waved their sou'westers and shouted, "Hurrah, *Fram*, Godspeed!"

By July 12 the *Fram* was at Tromso, and loaded reindeer cloaks, Lapp moccasins, and dried reindeer flesh. The first snow met them there, a gale and driving sleet. On to the North Cape, and then to the last town of Norway, Vardo on the Barents Sea. And here again, the fjords teemed with boats, flags waved, salutes were fired, and a band with a big new drum named the *North Pole* received the explorers, and there was a sumptuous banquet of farewell.

One last service was performed for the *Fram*. Divers cleaned her bottom of mussels and weeds so that she might go forward speedily. Again they took off, and now there was the last sight of Norway, lovely, quiet, and cool in the hazy morning. Nansen watched the land fade out. "I wonder what will happen to her and to us," he thought, "before we again see Norway rise up over the sea."

They headed now for Yugor Strait where they were to stop to pick up teams of Siberian sledge dogs. A German by the name of Trontheim was bringing these dogs. For four days, they steamed through fog, the endless stubborn fog of the Arctic.

Within a few days they saw the plains of northern Asia. The ship steamed into the Strait between rocky shores on which were a few desolate and weather-beaten buildings, a few tents and small houses. A boat now approached from land, and in a few minutes a man in European dress boarded the *Fram*. He was followed by a number of strange figures, heavily bearded, and wearing caps and long heavy robes of reindeer skin.

"Are you Trontheim?" asked Nansen.

"Yes, and we have the sledge dogs for you."

At Nansen's invitation the curious party sat down to supper, and Trontheim told how he had brought the dog caravan across northern Siberia up here to the top of the world to meet Nansen. "You cannot imagine the difficulties," Trontheim said. "We have been on the way for three months. We came through the foothills of the Ural mountains and across the tundras. We started with forty dogs and 9600 pounds of dried fish for their food. The tundra dwellers and their reindeer brought us."

Trontheim laughed and then continued. "We were a notable sight, forty dogs, four hundred fifty reindeer, and their owners, men, women, and children. We traveled over the plains by day and pitched tents at night. When we met other tundra dwellers, we stopped and drank tea with them in their tents. You may be sure we told our story. The people were greatly interested. They could not believe that the dogs were really going to the North Pole."

Trontheim looked at his companions, the men in the reindeer-skin coats. They nodded and laughed like children. "We went slow," they said. "Many reindeer have babies."

"I was often worried," continued Trontheim. "I was uncertain whether we would make the Strait in time to meet your ship. But it has turned out well. You will find the dogs in good condition."

After supper, the party landed, and Nansen went to see the dogs. They were long haired, some were snow white, and had likable, good-natured faces. It was time for their evening meal, and they swallowed raw fish ravenously.

In the next few days, Nansen explored the tundra country around Yugor Strait. Along the shores the water was ice free, but on the horizon, it was white and frozen. The land was all plains and low ridges, covered with a brownish-green carpet of moss and tiny Arctic flowers, one and two inches high. Nansen admired these tiny flowers, miniature yellow poppies, saxifrage, forget-me-nots, and little forests of tiny bluebells.

"They take the fancy captive," he said.

Some of the birds were as interesting to Nansen as the tiny flowers. One day he saw snow owls resting on a stone heap. They looked quite ghostly, silent, white, and motionless. At the end of these walks of exploration, Sverdrup usually built a fire of driftwood and made "glorious" coffee. The men then stretched out at their ease, and Sverdrup told story after story.

Other days the men took trial runs with the dogs, and had difficulty in learning to control the wild strong creatures. They went to a religious festival in the Russian church. Families came in from the tundras with reindeer teams, and the women wore fine brilliantly colored dresses, skirts with many tucks, and big bows at the end of their plaits of hair.

At last, on August 5, the winds were favorable for sailing. A south wind was blowing the ice northward in the Kara Sea. Sverdrup was optimistic. "The water will be clear all the way to the New Siberian Islands," he said.

By night the *Fram* got up steam; the dogs were brought on board with great noise and confusion, and again the *Fram* was off.

The last link with land was now broken. The ship steamed out into the mists, bound for the New Siberian Islands, the Arctic Ice Pack, and a tiny mathematical point at the very top of the world.

CHAPTER 5

WALLS OF ICE

The *Fram* steamed into the Kara Sea. A strange arctic hush and misty light were over everything. She passed skerries, and islets, and the men saw bears, reindeer herds, seal, and walrus. One day they saw a white fox enjoying life, taking wonderful leaps on the ice. On September 11, they came on a herd of walruses lying on an ice floe. The huge animals waddled to the edge of the ice and looked up at the ship with their great weird faces.

"Good gracious, what a lot of meat!" exclaimed Juell, the *Fram's* cook.

The men shot some of the creatures, and the rest went off roaring, and bellowing, and sending up clouds of spray.

On a dreamlike evening, when the sky was yellow and gold, the *Fram* passed Cape Chelyuskin, the most northerly point of Siberia. Nansen called for a celebration and gave a toast. "Skoal, my lads, and be glad we've passed Chelyuskin."

Northward—steadily northward, and at last, on September 22, the *Fram* entered the ice pack and was frozen in the drifting ice. "We must come out on the other side of the Pole," said Nansen. "Two years if we have luck, perhaps three. The ship is strong and can survive the ice, and I believe in the currents. The thing now is to get the ship ready and all the equipment set up properly. If the ship can survive the ice pressures, the life will be comfortable and safe. It may even be dull and monotonous."

It was a bleak world that Nansen looked out upon. As far as he could see in all directions were levels of ice. As he surveyed this dead world through his telescope, the only sign of life was one seal far out in open water. So there they were, beginning the adventure with the ice, many long miles from land and people. They must now depend entirely upon themselves to survive, and upon the currents for their movement.

There were many questions in Nansen's mind. How fast would they move northward and westward? How near to the Pole would the arctic currents bear them? Could the *Fram,* though so strongly built, withstand the terrible grinding and piling up of the ice floes during the times of storm? Or might she, too, like the *Jeanette* be crushed like the most fragile eggshell? If she were crushed, could the men take the equipment and escape and make their way with the dogs back to land? Could they live in the cold and could they find food? Soon the sun would be gone and the dreaded arctic night would come. There would be long months of darkness or pale moonlight. Could they keep their lights burning so that the ship could be a cheerful and bright spot in all the arctic night? So small a thing, yet so necessary for work and for cheer.

Only time could answer all the questions.

The thing now was work. First, the ship's engine. Each part was taken out, oiled, and laid away for the winter.

Amundsen did this. He tended each part as lovingly as if it were a child, and when the men teased him for all the loving care, he answered: "It's all very well for you to talk, but there's not such another engine in the world, and it would be a sin and a shame not to take good care of it."

The men set up workshops for all the necessary kinds of work. They set up a janitor's shop, a shoemaker's shop where each man might cut his own boots from a pattern of thick wood for soles and canvas for the tops. There was a place to care for sails and rigging, a place to melt fresh-water ice for the cooking, and drinking, and washing. There was a tin-smith's shop where the first job was the making of a huge pail for melting ice. One man was a watchmaker, and his work would be to keep all the watches in order.

One of the most interesting of the first jobs was the making of a small windmill. This windmill was set up on the foredeck of the ship. When it was finished, it would drive the dynamo and create power so that the ship could have electric lights. This small windmill became one of the best loved of all the devices that the men made. It looked whirling and cheerful, and because of it, even in the midst of the black arctic night, the ship was lighted up. Each man in his cabin had his own light to read by, and when the men went out on the ice for hunting and exploring, they would always come back to the *Fram* as though she were a star.

After the jobs that had to do with daily living were done, the men turned to the work of setting up scientific equipment. Instruments for measuring temperatures of the water, its depth, its degree of saltness, the amount of electricity in the air, observation of formation of the ice, currents of water beneath it, the collection and examination of such animal life as could be found in the northern seas, soundings, and dredgings.

The regular observation of the aurora borealis was also one of these duties. This aurora was so fascinating and splendid that in addition to the scientific reports of it, Nansen frequently wrote long descriptions in his diary. These lights can be seen at some time in most of the lands north of the equator. The farther north one goes, the greater they increase in wonder and variety. As Nansen watched, the lights assumed myriads of forms, colors, patterns, and movements. Sometimes the entire sky was a dome of delicate and dreamlike color, blue at the top, shading down into green, and lilac, and violet. Up in the blue were the friendly stars, and in the south a gold yellow moon with light golden clouds skimming over it. Then all at once, the aurora borealis would shake a veil of glittering silver over the whole sky. The veil would change to yellow, then to green, and to red. Then it would all melt away in the moonlight.

One afternoon in October after the *Fram* had been frozen in for three weeks, the ice was restless. There were groans and cracks and a high, plaintive moaning. The sounds increased as the afternoon wore on, growing and swelling like organ tones and then dying away. At the same time the ship trembled and shook and rose a little by fits and starts as though being gently lifted up.

"Ice pressure," said the men. "Look, the ice is piling up."

"What a squeeze!"

"We take it well," said another. "Look, how it lifts the boat."

In a little while, this first pressure ceased, and in the evening the ice walls fell away, and the *Fram* stood in open water. There was soft moonlight, and everything looked calm and quiet. The windmill turned lazily against the moon, and the whole scene was reassuring like a quiet picture, black and light and silent.

"A night made for sleep, boys," said one of the men. "The ice pack found us strong and drew back her fangs."

"I think it's early for the pressures," Nansen answered. "With luck we can hope to escape for several weeks. All the same I'll feel better when I see that we can take it."

"We are not like the *Jeanette*. We'll ride in the ice as in a cradle," said one.

"I hope we won't have to put it to the test, yet," answered Nansen. "We have further preparations to make. We must be ready at all times to leave the ship with sufficient provisions in case the ice is too much for us."

With these thoughts, he went to his cabin and slept.

The *Fram* rocked in the black water. The dogs tied on the deck slept in a heap. There was wonderful moonlight, white and strange. The hours of the night passed. All at once, in the early morning, at the time of the tidal wave, from far off over the open water and fields of ice floes, there came a low roar like the distant rumbling of an earthquake. It came closer and closer to the *Fram* until within a few minutes the whole moonlit world around her echoed with thunder. The ice floes, some of them ten to fifteen feet thick, were tossed about like feather weights. They began to pile up and push in thick walls toward the *Fram*. Even in the tremendous roar, there came sharper explosions as though giants were firing off giant cannons.

The men were all on deck, and the dogs were moaning. The ice came on. It drove against the *Fram* in a tremendous

228

thrust. Wham, crash, and roar! The men felt the mighty squeeze of the arctic ice pack, and even through the hurly-burly, heard the quivering of the ship.

Could any ship, however strongly built, hold out? The ice thrusts continued. Push, and push, and crash, and roar! All the world was thunder. Slowly the men felt the *Fram* lift up. Beneath her rounded hull, ice drove against ice and piled up in fourteen-foot-high walls. The groaning pack crashed, but the ship, pushed up above it, was sound and whole. Then, just as the disturbance began, growing from a moaning far away to thunder, so it diminished and died away again until the sounds were faint and far-off as though a spirit were wailing out on the ice fields.

"Whew!" said Johansen. "I can't believe it, but we're here. The *Fram is* whole. Only God knows how it can be possible."

The others were silent. Nansen went at once to inspect the ship. It was unbelievable that she could take such pressures. However, he was not able to find any sign of break. After awhile, as the ice continued to grow quiet, he went out to look around. He could see clearly in the moonlight. Walls of ice floes were in ridges ten to fourteen feet high. In between, the ice appeared unbroken and smooth. When he returned, he was content. "We've come through the first test," he said at breakfast. "The *Fram* behaved like a hero."

The men were jubilant. They ate a hearty breakfast which consisted of bread, cheese, corned beef, bacon, anchovy-roe, oatmeal biscuits, orange marmalade, and coffee. After the breakfast of the men, the dogs also celebrated the fact of being alive. They had dog biscuit and half a stockfish and then a jubilant run on the ice.

CHAPTER 6

A BOLD NEW PLAN

The days and weeks passed, November and December. The moon went round the sky and lighted up the snow and ice world. On board the ship, because of the windmill, lights always burned. It was a strange and dreamlike existence lived in moonlight and arctic stillness. The ship was moving northwest with the ice, yet the movement was so slow that it was like a snail's pace. Nansen's diary reflected the dreaminess, beauty, and monotony.

"O Arctic Night—how tired I am of thy cold beauty! I long to return to life. Let me home again, as conqueror or as beggar; what does that matter? But let me get home to begin life anew.

"The aurora borealis is burning in wonderful colors and bands of light over the whole sky. . . . Thousands of stars sparkle in the blue firmament among the northern lights. On every side, the ice stretches endless and silent into the night. The rime-covered rigging of the *Fram* stands out sharp and dark against the shining sky."

Christmas came, and the Christmas feast. The men had oxtail soup, fish pudding with potatoes and melted butter,

230

roast of reindeer with peas, French beans, potatoes, cranberry jam, cloudberries with cream, cake and marchpane.

A white dog named Kvik had puppies, thirteen of them. She had a furlined box to keep them warm in the 54 degrees of frost. These puppies soon would be tumbling and frolicking over the ship, bringing noise and playfulness to the dead world of the ice.

New Year's Day was an even greater celebration than Christmas. The weather was beautiful, cold and clear. Again there was a feast. At midnight, they ate pineapple, figs, cakes, and toddy. So the first six months in the ice ended, and the year 1893.

Nansen went to his berth. "Now the new year is here," he wrote in his diary. "One must prepare to wrestle with it. Attainment is far off. The time will be long, and many difficulties lie ahead. Well, we shall see. Till now I have lived under a lucky star. Is its light to be darkened? I am superstitious, no doubt, but I believe in my star."

During the fall, at the beginning of the second year in the ice, Nansen was disappointed at the distances covered. He wrote in his diary:

"When I make the calculation, it is really, to be honest, pretty discouraging."

He talked to Sverdrup, and the two men saw that at the present rate of drift it would take the *Fram* seven or eight years to get through the Polar Sea. A further disappointing fact was that they were too far south to get near the Pole. Nansen began to think of making a dash for the Pole on skis, taking one companion, and going with sledges and dogs. The *Fram* could then continue the observations and reports, and the two men could extend the explorations to the Pole itself.

Nansen talked over the idea with the men, and they all thought it could be worked out. The best time to go would probably be at the end of the winter. The distance to the Pole would be shortest at that time, approximately five hundred miles.

"We can make it in about fifty days," Nansen said. "That is, if the ice is reasonably smooth. The return journey will be easier with the lighter loads. Of course we can not count on finding the ship again, but we can make our way south to Franz Josef Land and will have no difficulty, I think, in finding a fishing boat in the summer that will get us home in the autumn."

Nansen chose as his companion, Hjalmar Johansen. Sverdrup wanted to go, but he was captain of the ship and could not leave. Johansen was a famous athlete, an excellent ski-runner. He was brave, resourceful, and cheerful.

The preparations for the trip were now begun. Nansen and Johansen moved out on the ice and slept in two sleeping bags in their tent. They found this arrangement too cold, so tried a double bag made of adult reindeer-skin. This they found better. They began to take long practice runs in the moonlight, and both men enjoyed these greatly. For clothes, the men at first tried wolfskins, but when they walked distances in them and at the same time pulled heavy loads, they found the clothes too heavy and hot. The moisture from their bodies clung to the furs until the suits were like armor. They finally decided on two woolen shirts, a thick jersey-and-camel's-hair coat. Felt caps with two hoods for varying degrees of cold, woolen drawers, knickerbockers,

232

They were off for the Pole!

a suit of cotton canvas to keep out the wind. Their shoes were made of skin from the hind legs of the reindeer buck, warm, flexible, and strong. Their gloves were of wolfskin, and underneath them, they wore wool mittens, neither having divisions for the fingers.

They took a tent of strong undressed silk; for heating and cooking, a Swedish gas-petroleum lamp called the Primus. In addition to these things, they had guns, instruments to determine position, kayaks made of light frames covered with sealskin, and sails for the sledges. The food required the most careful planning. They took dried and pulverized meat and fish, flour that had been steamed so that it was already cooked and needed only to be warmed, dried boiled potatoes, and dried breads. They would take 2100 pounds of food and provisions, twenty-eight dogs, and three sledges.

By the end of February, all was ready. Nansen was pleased. "Now, at last, the brain can get some rest, and the work for the legs and arms can begin," he said.

On March 14 they finally got off. What a stirring and fearful moment it was! Two men were off—bound for the Pole, five hundred miles away! Their lives now depended on their strength, and on their cheerful and resourceful minds.

Days and distances lay ahead. The first day was long. The ice was uneven; the sledges frequently capsized because of their heavy loads and were righted only with great difficulty. The two men stopped at six o'clock. They had made just nine miles, and it seemed to them already, at the end of the first day, as though they had been always walking and pushing on through snow and ice. The temperature was —45F. They put up the tent, filled the cooker with ice, lighted the small flame, and then while they waited for the ice to melt, they crawled into the sleeping bag to get warm. Supper was *fiskegraten,* made of fish meal, flour, and butter. After the food, they had a drink made of whey powder and hot water.

"It's wonderfully comforting," Nansen said. "I feel the warmth to the ends of my toes."

After supper, they crept down into the bag again, buckled the flap over their heads, and soon were asleep. But even in dreams, they went on grinding away at the sledges, and driving the dogs always to the north. Once Nansen woke with a start as Johansen called out in his sleep, "Pan, Barrabas, Klapperslanger—get on, you devils you! Go on, you brutes! Sass, sass!"

Outside the dogs lay in a heap on the ice, and the snow blew over them and around the small silk tent.

The first week went fairly well. But then the ice grew rougher and rougher; pressure ridges piled up twenty and thirty feet high, and the constant climbing and lifting of the sledges was work to tire giants. At night the men were often so tired that while they were eating their supper, they went to sleep with their spoons in their hands. Their clothes became an armor of ice during the day, and at night in the sleeping bags, they thawed out and were like wet bandages. The bag became their dearest friend.

"Into it quick," said Nansen at the end of each day. "We can warm up while supper cooks."

There they would lie, shivering and waiting, but when the supper was ready, it was wonderfully hot and magnificently delicious and well worth the time of waiting.

Northward, northward, always northward—grinding on, and at the end of the day, the silk tent and the dear bag, and the Primus singing cozily. At night, more and more frequently, the two men dreamed of Norway. Nansen saw clearly his home, Eva, and Baby Liv. These dreams were so vivid that it was always a shock to wake up shivering in the silk tent on the drift ice in the Arctic. The ice grew constantly worse, full of ridges and newly-frozen lanes. When they took observations for position, the readings were enough to break their hearts. The drift had carried them south; they had gone north scarcely at all in spite of all the toiling. They continued on until April 6. Nansen began to see that they must turn back.

"We cannot hope to make the Pole under present ice conditions," he said.

The next day he went forward alone on skis to survey the ice. He climbed the highest hummock that he could find, but all that he could see to the north was ugly ice and towering ridges. The decision to turn around was difficult, but once made, the men were cheerful. Each knew that at the present moment he stood on the northern-most point he would probably ever see.

"At least we can celebrate," said Nansen.

They put up the silk tent and the Norwegian flag, and prepared a banquet of lobscouse, bread and butter, dry chocolate, whortleberries, and their hot whey drink. "Now, into the dear bag," said Nansen when they finished. They crawled in, and each dreamed of the south, of Norway, home, and beautiful things. The sun woke them, shining cheerfully through the walls of the tent.

They now turned south. For three days, weather and ice

were good. Then it was the old story, ridges and hummocks and bitter weather. The bag became their only friend, and all the day they longed for the time to crawl into it. Sometimes when they slept, the ice pressures began, and it was like sleeping on an earthquake. All of April passed. They constantly scanned the horizon for sight of land, but there was never anything to be seen but ice and more ice endlessly. On May 17, Norwegian Constitution Day, they tied flags on the sledges in honor of the day and went forward bravely. On the same day, there was another excitement. Nansen heard a sound like huge regular breathing, and when he investigated, he found a lane of water and a whole school of whales breathing. On May 20, they spent the entire day in the bag because of a frightful blowing snowstorm. Then all of May was gone, and still there was no sight of land.

Snow, snow, and impenetrable mist. They had to shoot the dogs as they failed and could no longer do the work. This shooting was one of the hardest things for the men.

Nansen's diary reports the difficulties:

"June 5 We cannot have much farther to go.

"June 11 No sign of land in any direction and no open water.—We do not know where we are, and we do not know when this will end. Meanwhile our provisions are dwindling day by day, and the number of our dogs is growing seriously less. Shall we reach land while we yet have food, or shall we, when all is said, ever reach it?

"June 14 Three months since we left the *Fram*. A quarter of a year have we been wandering in this desert of ice, and here we are still.

"June 16 Yesterday was as bad as it well could be— the surface enough to make one desperate—I lie awake at night by the hour racking my brain to find a way out of our difficulties.

"June 27 The same monotonous life, the same wind, the same misty weather, and the same cogitations as to what the future will bring. There was a gale from the north last night, with a fall of hard granular snow, which lashed against the tent walls.

"July 3 Why write again? What have I to commit to these pages? Nothing but the same overpowering longing to be home and away from this monotony."

Then suddenly came the thing most longed for. On July 24, Nansen wrote:

"At last the marvel has come to pass—land, land! and after we had almost given up our belief in it."

CHAPTER 7

A CURIOUS MEETING

In the clear air, the land looked near, a day's march at most. But it took thirteen days to reach it, thirteen days of going over the ice and paddling in the two kayaks. One day they had a misadventure which almost took Johansen's life. An enormous bear came up and threw himself on Johansen. Nansen hurried to the kayak for his gun and was trying to pull it out when he heard Johansen say quietly, "You must look sharp if you want to be in time." Nansen got the barrel cocked, and shot, and the bear fell dead. The bear had come up so quietly in the fog that not even the dogs had heard him.

When they came closer to the land, there was open water, and it was a great pleasure to exchange the toil over the ice for gliding in open water. The land looked wonderfully beautiful to the two weary men.

"But where are we?" Nansen kept asking. "Can it really be Franz Josef Land?"

They landed on the evening of August 13, and for the first time in two years felt the earth under their feet. The coastal strip was almost free of snow and ice. There were black boulders and real stretches of sand. Nansen jumped from rock to rock and shouted out his delight. And when he found, in a sheltered nook between stones, some moss and flowering poppies, he could not get over the wonder of green and growing things. The ice began again only a little way up the shore, but there was the miracle. They ran up the Norwegian flag; it waved out over the first bare land. They prepared a banquet, lobscouse, and the last of the dried potatoes, and ate them in the tent and all the while kicked the bare land grit beneath their feet and marvelled.

"We sleep with no ice melting beneath us tonight," said Nansen. "I don't know where we are, but it's land. We'll explore in the morning. We must be somewhere on Franz Josef Land. With luck, we can get home by summer's end."

In the morning, when they explored, this land appeared to Nansen as the most lovely spot on all the face of the earth. There was a flat beach that was pleasant and easy to walk upon. Up on the cliffs were clouds of birds, and on the beach near them, snow buntings twittered cheerfully. After a while, Nansen and Johansen went out in the kayaks and paddled along the shore to continue their survey. The interior was all snow-covered. Huge bearded seals came up around the kayaks and gazed with great eyes. Then they went splashing off, blowing and diving and tumbling over so that the water foamed around them.

Nansen laughed. "It's good to see playfulness," he said. The day went well, and Nansen was optimistic about their good prospects. That night the sun, though misted over, stayed in the sky and gilded the world rose and gold, and they paddled along in the dreamy light.

"It's like being in a gondola on the Grand Canal," said Nansen.

The weather continued fair. Then on August 29, a howling winter storm came up; the ice packed all up the coast in ridges and hummocks. It was impossible to do anything but lie in the tent and listen to the wind howl, and finally to come to the bitter knowledge that the arctic winter was too close, and that the only possible thing to do was to hole in like bears and hope to get off in the spring and get south to the settlements.

"All we can do," said Nansen with resignation, "is to get a hut built. We can find stone and moss. Then after that we must collect the winter's food and fuel."

They began by hunting walrus. Some of the huge goblin-like creatures had come up on the shore ice. When Nansen went out with his gun, one of the monsters turned its round eyes upon him and gazed in astonishment. Nansen shot it easily. It would furnish piles of meat, blubber, and a tough skin for the roof of the hut. While they cut up the walrus, a whole school of white whales came blowing and breathing and gamboling in the open water.

Nansen took the shoulder blade of the walrus and, fastening it to a wood staff, made a spade to be used in building the hut. The two men worked, building and hunting walrus and bears until the food was piled up for the winter, and the hut was snug. The hut when it was finished was ten feet long, six feet wide, and six feet high. The entrance was a tunnel of ice and snow built in the manner of the Eskimos. Nansen made a lamp of flat pieces of German silver turned up on the edges. In this he put blubber, and for wicks, cut strips of the bandages from the medicine bag. For beds, the two men piled up rocks, covered them with bearskins and the sleeping bag. They built a hearth in one corner for the cooking fire. The cooking itself would be simple, bear's broth in the morning, and bear's steak at night. Before the winter would pass, they would eat nineteen bears. Sometimes with the meat, they ate pieces of blubber. They liked the browned pieces left after they fried out the blubber to get oil for the lamps. They called these little browned pieces "cakes" and wished they had some sugar to put on the top.

October 15 came, and it was time for the sun to go. Their third arctic night began, the third time of dark and cold. Two men in a hut! Dark, cold and empty time! "We'll take turns at being cook," said Nansen. "It will help to divide the time."

The light of the oil lamps was poor and flickering. The temperature rarely rose above zero. Nansen lay on the floor in the bag and tried to write up his diaries. It was hard to do. When he touched the paper, it turned black and greasy. "I long for ink and white paper," he said to Johansen. "I can scarcely read what I write on these black pages."

They went out each day for exercise, two black figures in the arctic dark, running up and down to keep warm. When the moon came, the appearance of their shadow world changed and became a fairyland of shining white.

The snow whirled, and the winds blew, and the aurora borealis danced like spirits over the sky. It was a strange existence. How they longed for books, any print at all on any subject to bring in the world of men. Nansen had an old almanac, and though he had read it so many times that he knew it by heart, it was a great comfort to him. He pored over it, reading by the flickering lamp, fed by the walrus blubber.

One night, Nansen looked up from this black almanac.

"Do you know," he said, "some things I have learned for good. I shall always set store by the good things of life, books, food, drink, clothes, shoes, house, home, neighbors."

"Yes," answered Johansen fervently. "If we make the ship in the spring, do you think they'll have potatoes and bread? Will there be sugar and butter?"

"Think of shirts," said Nansen, "soft wool trousers, and clean socks and slippers. And a Turkish bath."

The two men sat up in the sleeping bag. They talked of a shop full of clean new clothes, racks and racks of things spread out. All were clean and soft and would not stick to the body.

"Ugh, these rags," said Johansen. He pulled the oily clinging shirt from his wrist. "Add soap to your list of the good things of the world."

The problem of cleanliness was one of the hardest for the two explorers. Their bodies and their clothes were so heavy with grease that water had no effect upon them. They scoured their bodies with moss and sand, or rubbed them with bears' blood and oil and then scrubbed this off with moss. They boiled their clothes in the pot hour after hour, but when they took them out, they found that they were just as filled with grease as when they put them in. The best way was to boil them, and then, while they were still warm, scrape them all over with a knife. Each man held his garment between his teeth and his left hand, and as he held it stretched tightly in this way, he scraped with the right hand. It was simply incredible how much fat came out. This fat was then added to the fuel supply.

The curious life continued. February, March, and April passed, and it was time to prepare for the summer march.

"Man is ingenious if there is no shop next door," said Nansen one night. He was sitting in the bag, near the small wick light, and was unravelling strands of thread from their heavy provision bags. Both men had cut new clothes from their blankets and were sewing them together with these threads. They made socks and gloves of bearskin, and a new sleeping bag also of bearskin. For these last, they had to kill bears and prepare the skins carefully.

By May the weather was favorable, and on the nineteenth, they left the tiny hut. Nansen wrote out the story of their lives in the hut and he put this record in a brass tube and suspended it from the ceiling.

"Someone will find it someday," he said.

"I can't believe we're starting home again," said Johansen.

"We'll make it this summer," said Nansen.

The familiar life began again. On some days they made excellent progress. They tied sails to the sledges and the wind drove them skimming over the ice. Other days they could not go forward at all through the ice ridges and water lanes. One day the expedition almost came to an end. They tied the kayaks to an edge of ice and went ashore to stretch their legs a little. Suddenly Johansen shouted, "I say, the kayaks are adrift."

Nansen ran to the ice edge, pulled off his jacket and boots, and jumped into the water. The kayaks were well out and were being carried rapidly by the wind. All that they had was in the kayaks; if they were lost, the men could not possibly survive. They had not even a knife between them. Nansen put every effort into the swimming. When he tired, he turned over and swam on his back. Both legs and arms were stiffening and losing feeling, and he knew that in a short time he would not be able to move them. But the distance was growing less, and at last he was able to catch the edge of the kayak. After a while, he threw one leg up and managed to tumble in. He was numb all over and only with the greatest effort could he paddle back. He shivered and his teeth chattered. Johansen had the bag ready and when Nansen crept into it, he piled the sails and all that he had over him. Nansen fell asleep in complete exhaustion. When he awoke, Johansen had hot soup ready.

There was one other terrible day when a herd of angry walrus attacked the light kayaks. The men had to beat them off, fearing all the time lest one of the sharp horns would rip open the frail boats. Nansen's kayak had a short gash, but he managed to get it mended before serious harm was done.

Then one day in the middle of June, their luck changed. Good things began to happen, and they were so incredible that Nansen himself had difficulty in believing in their wonderful fantastic fortune. It began about noon on June 17. It was Nansen's day to be cook. Johansen was resting in the bag, and Nansen had built up the fire, and cut up the meat and put it in the pot. He sat down, pulled off one boot, and was about to crawl into the bag to wait for the meat to cook, when he noticed that the heavy artic mist which had been thick over the island for several days was rising.

"I'll have a look around while it's clear," he said. He pulled on the boot and went off a little ways inland. Coming upon a large snow hummock, he climbed up on it to make his survey. Ahead stretched the snow land, and up the coast, the black and jagged cliffs covered with thousands of birds. The sight was majestic and mysterious, a mighty landscape, tremendous, wide, and empty.

At the very moment when Nansen thought he was alone on top of the world, he heard a sound like the barking of a dog. He strained his ears to listen, and this time heard only the bubbling sounds of the thousands of birds on the cliff. Then unmistakably came the barking again.

Nansen turned and shouted to Johansen. "Johansen, Johansen, there are dogs inland."

Johansen started up from the bag. "Dogs," he shouted back. "No, that is not possible."

Nansen went back to the fire and the two men ate hastily. "Could it be the English expedition to Franz Josef Land that was planned when we left?" Nansen puzzled. It seemed hardly possible. While Johansen stayed with the kayaks to keep them from drifting off, Nansen set out inland. Not far from the snow hummock, he saw tracks in the snow which looked like the tracks of a dog.

"They are too big for a fox, and too small for a wolf," Nansen thought. "Can it really be that all our toil and trouble and sufferings are to end here?"

It seemed incredible, yet—

Again the sound of a dog's barking came clearly. Suddenly Nansen thought he heard a shout, a strange human voice. His heart beat, and the blood rushed to his head. He ran up on a hummock and shouted with all the strength of his lungs. Then, as he stood with pounding heart, looking down the ice ridges, he saw home and Eva waiting there, and, only after the swift vision, a dog, and farther off, behind him, a man.

Nansen waved his hat and went swiftly. He recognized Mr. Jackson, the English explorer whom he had once seen. Jackson extended his hand. "How do you do?"

Then the man in dirty rags, all black with oil and soot, with uncombed hair and shaggy beard, his face covered with fat and soot which even a knife had tried in vain to remove, held out his hand to a civilized European, neatly dressed, well groomed, and smelling of soap.

"Jackson, I'm immensely glad to see you."

"Thank you. I also."

"Have you a ship here?"

"No, my ship is not here."

"How many are there of you?"

"I have one companion at the ice edge."

Suddenly Jackson stopped and looked Nansen full in the face. Then he said quickly, "Aren't you Nansen?"

"Yes, I am."

"By Jove! I am glad to see you."

Then he seized Nansen's hand and shook it again and again, his whole face a smile of welcome. "Where have you come from now?" he asked.

Nansen told some of his story while Jackson marveled that men could manage such a life. "I congratulate you most heartily," he said.

In a few hours, Nansen and Johansen were in the English camp. They had baths, food, clothes, and letters.

"Dream, dream of home and beauty!" wrote Nansen that night in the strange, greasy, black diary. "Dream the golden dream."

They reached Norway in August. They landed at Vardo Haven, and were off to the telegraph station with messages to be sent out to the world. As they went, no one recognized them. "We still look like pirates," laughed Nansen in excitement. The only being that took notice of them was a cow which stopped in the middle of the street and stared in astonishment. Nansen had an impulse to pat the cow. "She is so delightfully summery," he said. "I feel as though I really am in Norway."

In the telegraph office, the man in charge picked up the messages. When he read the signature, his face lighted.

"Welcome home!" he said heartily. "Congratulations!"

Then he went to the lady clerk at the table and pointed out Nansen's signature. Both came and stood beaming. "It will take several days and nights to get all the messages out," he said, "but we will do it as fast as possible."

After the wires were sent, Nansen's first questions were of the *Fram*. In spite of the brave wire, he was worried. There was no news, but just one week later, the report of her arrival came. She had come out of the ice on the day that Nansen had landed in Norway.

One can imagine the celebration given in Norway for the explorers. In Oslo, the capital, one hundred and thirty steamers decked in flags escorted the *Fram* up the harbor. There was a salute of thirteen guns, followed by thirteen answering peals of thunder from the harbor fortress. There was a festival parade, and singing, and many speeches of tribute. The poet, Bjornson, gave one of the speeches.

"For it is true," he said, "that the work, the faith, and the self-control that a people wins in silence comes to light someday in a great deed, and then the great deed is just the same as though the whole people had attained its majority."

To the Norwegians, it was as Bjornson said. All of them had been allowed to share in a great adventure. Both adventure and hero were theirs.

CHAPTER 8

NANSEN'S GREATEST WORK

It was difficult settling to work again. Sometimes it seemed to Nansen that he would be stifled by talk and by crowds and that he must escape to great spaces, vast and silent. He looked well again. He regained the ruddy color that he had lost during the winter in the hut on Franz Josef Land. He lost some weight, grew harder. He was extraordinarily handsome, tall, dignified, and kindly. He wore fine wool clothes of his own design and never got over his fondness for their softness and quality. These clothes were cut like a close-fitting ski costume, and in cut and style, they became him well. People liked to turn and look at his strong well-built figure striding off down the streets of Oslo in the individually fashioned clothes.

He was a University professor again, in charge of a department of oceanography. This was a new department, an entirely new field. Nansen was the only one who had done much work in it. He worked with microscope and fine instruments and collected important data. As professor of oceanography he added greatly to man's knowledge of ocean tides and currents, of water temperatures, and their effects upon the climates of the land. He went on cruises of exploration and found new and extensive beds of fish so that the fishing industries of his country could be enormously expanded and new work and income could be given to the Norwegians.

He was so greatly respected that he was finally asked to help work out the political problems of his country. He worked for the League of Nations and for Norway's participation in it because he believed that nations must work together to solve their problems peacefully.

He wrote books, many of them. Among them is the magnificent story of the north pole trip in the *Fram,* called *Farthest North* which is one of the great adventure stories of all time. He also began a history of Northern explorations called *In Northern Mists.*

He built a fine and spacious house in the pine forest for his five children, and made a happy and interesting home for them. Although he never thought of himself as an artist, he made many unusual, bold, and dramatic pictures of the far North. He made a trip of exploration at the request of the Russian government along the northern coast of Siberia and made recommendations for future trading.

But the greatest of all the things that he did came near the end of his life. It was just after World War I. The people of Europe were poor and confused. There were so many different kinds of suffering that no one seemed to know how to begin to help. The League of Nations was meeting in Geneva, and Nansen was Norway's delegate. The representatives of the nations took up one problem after another. One of these was what could be done for the men who had been taken as prisoners during the war. In some cases, the countries that had taken the prisoners no longer existed, and there were camps of forgotten men who were ill, and without clothes, or money.

Some of these camps were in the far east of Russia, and in Siberia, such distances away that some of the men did not learn that the war was over for many years. The new Russian government had no records of many of these prisoners. As far as anyone knew, they had simply disappeared.

When the League of Nations committee asked Nansen to see what could be done for the prisoners of war, he asked many questions. How many prisoners were there? Was there money to do the investigating, to get food, clothes, and transportation? The answers to all the questions were, "No one knows."

In spite of all the difficulties, Nansen began to work. The tall, dignified and kindly Norseman was respected everywhere, and soon he was able to find help. He went first to Russia. He found the country struggling to establish her new kind of government. The Czar and the old officials new officers were all gone. The new leaders were suspicious of Europeans who had fought against them in their revolution.

"We no longer have records of the prisoners," the Russian official said at first. "We will not consider working with the League of Nations which is hostile to us."

"Work with me as an individual," Nansen answered. "Let me be the representative of each separate government."

The Russian officials were doubtful if that could be done.

"If you refuse, you will have on your conscience the lives of thousands of men," Nansen answered. "I do not believe that that is the wish of the new government."

Finally plans were made. The Russian government

251

agreed to send out two trains each week and to pay the expense of these trains while they were in Russian territory. Often it was hard for the Russians to find the prisoners. Camps had disappeared, and it was necessary for someone to go to the villages and ask questions. "Are there foreigners here?" Sometimes little groups would be found in this way, and would be loaded on the prisoner trains.

In a year and a half, Nansen had arranged for the homecoming of almost half a million prisoners. It is difficult to imagine the joy of so many men as they returned to their families who had given up all hope for them. Philip Noel Baker, the Englishman who had persuaded Nansen to undertake the great work wrote these words about him: "There is not a country on the continent of Europe where wives and mothers have not wept in gratitude for the work which Nansen did."

Nansen performed other tasks at the request of the League of Nations. Of these, the problem of the refugee children was the hardest of all. The children had lost their families and many were so little that they did not remember their names. Small babies had chewed up the identification tags that had been tied to them, so there was no possible way to find out where they belonged. Again Nansen and his helpers made arrangements. Most of the countries of Europe assumed the responsibility for the refugee children.

Another great task which Nansen did was to bring relief to Russia in the time of the terrible famine of 1921. Herbert Hoover directed the relief for the United States, and the amount done was incredibly great. The Russian Famine was so terrible and widespread that no one country could possibly relieve it. The harvest had failed in all the Volga

Valley and the southern Ukraine, and thirty-three million people were affected. As so many became weak and ill and susceptible to disease, epidemics of dysentery, cholera, and spotted typhus raged.

Nansen stood up in the Assembly and spoke with deep emotion. "Is it possible," he said, "that Europe can sit quietly and do nothing? I cannot believe it. I feel convinced that the people of Europe will compel the governments to reverse their decisions. . . . In this place I appeal to the governments, to the people of Europe, to the whole world, for their help. Hasten to act before it is too late to repent."

But even after the wonderful speech, Nansen's request was voted down. It was one of his worst defeats, and the tall man was bowed down by it. But then he took his case to other places. He went on a lecture tour all over Europe, and then to the United States, and everywhere told the story of the starving Russians. Many hearers wept, or left the hall because they could not bear to hear more. Nansen told of families who took the thatched roofs from their barns and houses, and ground up the old thatch into a powder for food. He said that all over southern Russia, there were the roofless buildings.

Once in the United States, after one of these talks, Nansen hurried to his car. An American reporter who looked after the tall bowed figure, stopped, gazed after him, and then said with respect and admiration: "The church towers bow down in the night as he drives by."

Many answered Nansen's pleas for help, and although the terrible Russian winter set in before supplies could be gotten to all the people, yet many were saved. Norway, Denmark, Sweden, England, Holland, France, and Italy sent aid. The United States supported two and a half million children. Herbert Hoover's American Relief worked constantly, and was excellently carried out. Nansen wrote of it: "In the whole history of the world, there is no humanitarian work that can be compared with the relief work organized by Hoover during and after the War, which had its climax here in Russia."

Nansen's great work continued as long as he lived. In 1922, he was given the wonderful Nobel peace prize which is awarded to one who in the opinion of the judges does the most to advance the cause of peace in the world. He divided this prize between Greek refugees, and some experimental agricultural stations in Russia which were helping the Russian people.

Fridtjof Nansen lived until 1930. The first part of his life, all the years of adventure and exploration, make a fascinating story to read. The last years, however, are even greater. But to tell the story of them is not possible. One would have to have a book about every one of the prisoners, every one of the refugees, of the refugee children, and the Russians who were saved. But as the first years revealed Nansen's strength, hardiness, incredible resourcefulness, courage, and patience, the last revealed a heart great enough to include all men, and a vision of a world in which men must learn to live together in friendship.

Once Nansen had written: "I see farther ahead a new world to be built, and I want to build it."

He had a great part in building it. While much remains to be done, the memory of such a one as Fridtjof Nansen inspires others to continue the task. After his death, at the last ceremony, the national anthem of Norway was sung.

How fitting the song of patriotism was! Nansen had always loved his land and worked for her, as explorer, as professor, as scientist. In his last years, he had worked for the most important thing of all, her responsible participation in the larger affairs of the larger world.

Norway is rightly proud of her great sons; Ole Bull going out as a gay troubador, Henrik Ibsen stirring up the peoples' thoughts, Edvard Grieg giving the world the music of Norway, and finally Fridtjof Nansen who did what they all must have dreamed of doing, leading Norway to play her greatest role.

Today Norway is no longer an isolated corner of the world, the land of poetic fjords and mountains that Ole Bull and Edvard Grieg talked about, but a modern nation fully participating in the life of the world and playing a noble and courageous part.

BIBLIOGRAPHY

In addition to numerous books on Norwegian history, literature and geography, the following books were used:

Brögger, W. C., and Rolfsen, Nordahl. *Fridtjof Nansen.* New York: Longmans, Green & Co., Ltd., 1896. 274 pp. $4.00.   O.P.
Bull, Sara. *Ole Bull: A Memoir.* Boston: Houghton Mifflin Company, 1883. 417 pp. $2.50.   O.P.
Finck, Henry T. *Edvard Grieg.* London: John Lane Company, 1906. 130 pp. $1.00.   O.P.
——— *Grieg and His Music.* New York: Dodd, Mead & Company, Inc., 1929. 242 pp. $3.00.   O.P.
Gosse, Edmund. *Henrik Ibsen.* New York: Charles Scribner's Sons, 1908. 200 pp. $1.50.   O.P.
Jaeger, Henrik. *Henrik Ibsen.* Chicago: A. C. McClurg & Co., 1890. 322 pp. $1.50.   O.P.
Johansen, David Monrad. Translated from the Norwegian by Madge Robertson. *Edvard Grieg.* New York: American-Scandinavian Foundation and Princeton University Press, 1938. 400 pp. $4.00.   O.P.
Jorgenson, Theodore. *Henrik Ibsen: A Study in Art and Personality.* Northfield, Minnesota: St. Olaf College Press, 1945. 550 pp. $3.50   O.P.
Koht, Halvdan. *Life of Ibsen* (2 vol.). Translated by Ruth Lima McMahon and Hanna Astrup Larsen. New York: American-Scandinavian Foundation with W. W. Norton & Company, Inc., 1931. Vol. 1, 304 pp.; Vol. 2, 341 pp. $7.50.   O.P.
Nansen, Fridtjof. *Eskimo Life.* London: Longmans, Green & Co., Ltd., 1893. 350 pp. $4.00.   O.P.
——— *Farthest North* (2 vol.). New York: Harper & Brothers, 1897. Vol. 1, 587 pp.; Vol. 2, 729 pp. $10.00.   O.P.
——— *The First Crossing of Greenland.* London: Longmans, Green & Co., Ltd., 1890. 464 pp. $2.50.   O.P.
Smith, Mortimer Brewster. *Life of Ole Bull.* New York: American-Scandinavian Foundation and Princeton University Press, 1943. 220 pp. $3.00.
Sörensen, Jon. *Saga of Fridtjof Nansen.* Translated from the Norwegian by J. B. C. Watkins. New York: American-Scandinavian Foundation, 1932. 372 pp. $4.50.   O.P.
Zucker, Adolf Edward. *Ibsen the Master Builder.* New York: Henry Holt and Company, Inc., 1929. 312 pp. $3.50.   O.P.

Periodical

Music Student. Vol. 8, No. 5, 1916. Published at 10 Carlton Terrace, Child's Hill, London, N. W.

DATE DUE

201-6503

Printed
in USA